GAME OF
THRONES
ON BUSINESS

Strategy, morality and leadership lessons from
the world's most talked-about TV show

TIM PHILLIPS AND REBECCA CLARE

infiniteideas

First published in 2015 by

Infinite Ideas Limited
36 St Giles
Oxford
OX1 3LD
United Kingdom
www.infideas.com

A CIP catalogue record for this book is available from the British Library

ISBN 978-1-908984-38-8

Printed in Spain

CONTENTS

INTRODUCTION

Bran: *"I hate your stories."*
Old Nan: *"I know a story about a boy who hated stories."*

If you've never watched *Game of Thrones*, you may be missing out on more than mere entertainment. A story of sex, swordfighting and ice monsters set in a fictional sort of medieval Europe might not be the most obvious place to head to when you're hoping to advance your career. It has many fans but equally high numbers of people will have been put off by the fact that it's set in a fantasy realm, contains gratuitous sex and gore and features characters with names that look like anagrams. And yes, in the wrong hands this tale could easily have become a ridiculously campy piece of soft porn with dragons but that's not what we have. Instead it is a thrilling and complex drama of ambition, deceit, bravery, folly, triumph and disaster. Which makes it an excellent source of tips on career building, leadership and how to do business.

Regardless of your feelings on dragons, with *Game of Thrones*, as with so much in life, you stay for the stories. And these stories can help us make sense of our own lives. As the biologist William Calvin explains in a 2006 paper on 'The emergence of intelligence': 'Our abilities to plan gradually develop from childhood narratives and are a major foundation for ethical choices, as we imagine a course of action, imagine its effects on others and decide whether or not to do it.' So, we do not learn by being told, but by doing and observing, and working out what happens next. We learn by creating a story out of experience. But, when we grow up and go to university and then get an office job, what does the world give us to make sense of life?

PowerPoint, that's what. PowerPoint is anti-story. We go into a room. Someone reads out thirty slides which all seem to be lists. Sometimes the lists magically appear, point by tedious point: as suspenseful as watching a tap drip. Sometimes the lists have little sublists, which have their own titchy sub-sublists. The titchy lists are in italics. No one tells you why. Sometimes there will be important diagrams which pretend they tell a story, but make no sense.

A proper story has what Chris Anderson, the man who created TED talks (and therefore a man who knows about storytelling) calls the 'aha moment': the pleasure when we work something out for ourselves, when we realize something without someone telling us it. The fog lifts.

Jokes have this structure, conversation has it, sport has it, walking into a bar and choosing a beer has it, and *Game of Thrones* has it in seven kingdoms. Presentations do not, because most of the people who write them don't bother to put it in. Which is why you'll learn far more about business from *Game of Thrones* than you will from a dozen teambuilding seminars. Mind you, you're probably going to have a problem convincing your boss your expenses claim for the box set is justified.

We enter the story during a period of upheaval. Recent history has seen a rebellion against the rule of the Targaryens, which had lasted for 300 years. Robert Baratheon beat the Mad King Aerys but his rule is far from secure. But this makes the tale particularly valuable for us. After all there's little entertainment to be had or indeed any lessons to be learned from peacetime. Tough times are when the mettle of those who wish to succeed is really tested and when leaders really prove themselves. It sorts the men from the boys. On one side are difficulties, challenges, potential death (or the business equivalent failure, possibly bankruptcy but you'll most likely keep your head), but this is when business gets most exciting. The potential rewards at the same time are great too. In *Game of Thrones* the winner aims to gain the throne; in business status, a sense of personal achievement and financial rewards usually result from success.

There are almost as many management styles and routes to success as there are leaders so it's well-nigh impossible to create a definitive book on career success. What we hope you'll find here is a guide to writing your own career story by looking at this most entertaining of tales in a new way.

1

LEAD TO SERVE

Jorah Mormont: *"You have a good claim, a title, a birthright, but you have something more than that … You have a gentle heart. You would be not only respected and feared, you would be loved. Someone who can rule and should rule. Centuries come and go without a person like that coming into the world."*

Daenerys may have been born with leadership in her blood but she's also had to work on her skills in this area. When we first see her she's a nervous, slouching girl, terrified of Khal Drogo and bullied by her brother. All she wants to do is go home, and when she says that she's not talking about leading an army to take the throne, she's simply talking about going back to somewhere safe so they can stop their wandering exile. Circumstances force her to change her behaviour and alter her ambition – "To cross the narrow sea and take back the Iron Throne". At least to begin with everything she does is focused on staying alive but gradually she realizes that she can do more than this. When her brother Viserys makes one too many attempts to dominate her on the grounds of his right to the throne and her status as merely the wife of a 'savage' she turns on him. He says her anger has woken the dragon (meaning the dragon in him) but actually he wakes hers as she says, "I am the wife of the great Khal and I carry his son inside me. The next time you raise a hand to me will be the last time you have hands." She realizes that even if Khal Drogo were to give Viserys an army he'd never be able to lead it or regain the throne of Westeros.

Daenerys is not motivated by a need for power but arguably by what she believes is best for her people – the 'small folk' at home who are sewing banners and praying for the return of Targaryen rule. In this manner she embodies the ideals of the servant-leader, an idea first written about by Robert Greenleaf in the 1970s, which suggested that the ideal leader is motivated by a need to serve – and they serve (a cause, the business, their people) best by leading. This is in stark contrast to a more self-first model of leadership where the leader's primary goal is to be in charge. Greenleaf argued that an organization functions better under a servant-leader than under the leader who puts his or her personal goals first. Daenerys' first motivation is to serve her people; she can do this best by ensuring that she instead of Viserys, the Lannisters or the Baratheons leads them.

The Faith of the Seven, the official religion of Westeros, worships a deity with seven aspects, which represent ideals. Of the three female aspects the maiden represents purity, love and beauty while the mother represents mercy, peace, fertility, childbirth and the strength of women. As the series progresses we see Daenerys make her transition from 'maiden' to 'mother'. She gains her true motherhood by losing her child and her husband and becoming the 'Mother of Dragons', but her mothering doesn't stop there. When she frees the slaves at Yunkai they carry her aloft chanting "Mhysa, Mhysa", which Missandei then explains means 'mother' in their language. Although unlike Daenerys in many other respects, current chancellor of Germany, Angela Merkel, is referred to affectionately by her people as 'Mutti' – Mummy. Although relatively uncharismatic, Merkel is clearly a leader who inspires love, somebody the German people feel is a safe pair of hands who has their best interests at heart. Daenerys freed the slaves; Merkel kept the German economy healthy throughout the recession and resultant Eurozone crisis.

Both Cat Stark and Cersei are strong women who would do anything for their children – as Cersei states, "Sometimes we go to extremes where our children are concerned". Cat defends Bran against a knife-wielding assassin at the cost of some very sliced-up hands. Just as servant leadership does not mean being servile, a motherly style of leadership does not mean being soft. A leader who is weak cannot defend her business against a rival and in internal dealings a manager who lets her employees do whatever they please soon finds them to be unmanageable. But a firm hand that is also caring inspires trust in people so that they follow you out of love. Susan Wojcicki, CEO of YouTube, owned by Google, sees herself as the 'Mom' of Google, referring to her management style (though she was also the first Googler to have kids), but former co-workers point out that this doesn't mean she's soft. She's renowned for being nice but as AOL chairman and CEO Tim Armstrong, who worked with her at Google, says 'underneath it, she's a real fierce competitor.' This shouldn't really come as a surprise – you're not going to get far at a company like Google simply by being 'nice' and since her promotion in February 2014 she's had to restructure, leading to the inevitable redundancies.

The mother style of leadership is not just for girls. To carry it off you need to be a real people person but if you get it right your employees will follow you anywhere, out of love not out of duty.

2

LEAD TO WIN

Tywin Lannister: *"Have you gone soft, Clegane? I always thought you had a talent for violence. Burn the villages, burn the farms. Let them know what it means to choose the wrong side."*

The mothering style of leadership is not for everyone – if mercy and peace don't work for you why not try your hand at the other extreme? Careful though, this route is not for the faint-hearted.

Hand of the King Tywin Lannister is ruler of the Seven Kingdoms in all but name. He's a pragmatist – in justifying murdering Robb Stark and his family at the wedding of Edmure Tully and Roslin Frey he says, "Explain to me why it is more noble to kill 10,000 men in battle than a dozen at dinner". Tywin is also a master strategist and most alpha of all the alpha males in this story. It's a constant source of irritation to him that he's surrounded by pussy-footing moralizers. Tywin's entirely justified belief in his own superiority makes him dictatorial, and brutal with underlings, foes and even his own children. Regretting that Tyrion is his issue, treating Cersei as a 'broodmare', telling Jaime it's about time he became a man, he makes no attempt to cover up his disappointment in any of them. He just wants them to do him, or more accurately the Lannister name, proud. He's been very successful, but never been king – but then only a 'fool' would believe the king was the most powerful man in Westeros. He has the strength and courage a good leader requires but has had to stand by and see a mad king succeeded by a drunk and then by a child because they had 'just' claims to rule. So he's constantly striving for more and impatient to achieve his goals – in this context you can see why he's frustrated by what he perceives as everybody else's uselessness.

In times of crisis a leader like Tywin has his merits. People need to be motivated to succeed but there isn't time for a teambuilding approach where everybody's needs and goals are taken into consideration. It's what management scientists Blake and Mouton termed 'produce or perish' in their managerial grid. In this grid they pitched concern for people against concern for production. The most successful companies will manage successfully to bring about high production levels while also creating high job satisfaction among their employees; other less successful companies will demonstrate different levels of both. Tywin's way aims for high 'production' but at a time of crisis, as leader of a new team, he doesn't have time to consider anything besides getting the job done. Sitting around trying to make sure everyone is happy in his or her role could mean they lose an advantage, a battle, the war. In the age of the servant-leader Tywin's style seems uncomfortably authoritarian and Victorian; so surely somebody who tried to run a business Tywin's way today wouldn't last long?

Well guess again. Apple founder Steve Jobs was one of the most successful entrepreneurs of all time. A few weeks after he died a frank biography authored by Walter Isaacson was published. The book was written at Jobs' behest and featured interviews not only with him but with colleagues, rivals and family members. Depending on your perspective Jobs comes across in the book as either single-minded and success oriented or a complete asshole. For example, at Apple's inauspicious launch of MobileMe, a subscription service that was supposed to sync a user's entire online existence in the cloud, Jobs humiliated the MobileMe employees in front of the entire auditorium for their failure to create a better product, saying, 'You should hate each other for having let each other down,' before firing the team leader on the spot. Despite this and other nasty tactics such as claiming staff members' good ideas as his own, he inspired great work in his employees and created a world-beating company producing iconic products. As his biographer says, talking of Jobs in the same breath as other entrepreneur assholes Edison, Ford and Disney, 'Long after their personalities are forgotten, history will remember how they applied imagination to technology and business.' Jobs has as many acolytes for his management style as detractors, with many a would-be entrepreneur using his style as their model for success.

But here we should strike a cautionary note; Jobs really was exceptional and because of this an exception to norms of management. Isaacson also notes that, 'He acted as if the normal rules didn't apply to him'. In most businesses Jobs' bullying style of management would lead to reduced productivity and creativity – it's hard to do your job well if you're spending most of your time worrying about being humiliated, belittled or sacked. It's something Douglas McGregor wrote about in his book *The Human Side of Enterprise* as a style of leadership motivated by 'Theory X'. This assumes that workers inherently dislike work and therefore need to be controlled, coerced and directed by management. But managing from this assumption tends to lead workers to behave in the way you expected them to – it's a self-fulfilling prophecy. After all, what's the point in trying to be creative and impress an unimpressable boss? (Its opposite theory, Theory Y suggests that people function best if they are given space to create, to develop and take responsibility for their work.)

Former British prime minister Gordon Brown proved the inadequacies of this style of leadership with his stapler-throwing antics. Brown had never won a general election, having inherited the role of prime minister from Tony Blair, who stepped down as leader of the Labour Party mid-way through a government in June 2007 (this can happen in the UK as parties, not leaders, are elected, the prime minister being the leader of the party that holds the most seats in the House of Commons). Having attained the office he'd always yearned for but realizing that he had a limited time to make his mark before the next general election in May 2010 one can see that he'd be in a hurry to get things done but that doesn't really excuse his treatment of his team. Brown allegedly had a bit of a temper, and had frequent tantrums, throwing phones, pens and staplers at staff. Unfortunately for the uncharismatic Brown this merely made him unpopular in his own party and led to further rumours and mockery in the British press. The point is that Steve Jobs could have been right here – when you are head and shoulders above the herd you can get away with a lot more than mere mortals; the normal rules really do not apply to you. So if you're planning to follow his lead you had better be sure you're either the richest man in the realm or a bona fide creative genius.

3

DON'T MIX BUSINESS AND PLEASURE

Tormund: *"I've seen you slip a shaft through a rabbit's eye at two-hundred yards. If that boy's still walking it's 'cause you let him go."*

When Jon Snow infiltrates the Wildling camp he falls for passionate warrior woman Ygritte. We all know no good can come of it – his feelings for her compromise his judgement, and eventually he has to choose between his Night's Watch brothers and her. While the outcome is rarely as devastating in business, failing to draw a line between your personal life and your work life is fraught with difficulty.

The Night's Watch oath includes a vow of celibacy for a very good reason – a romantic relationship complicates a man's life and the 'shield that guards the realms of men' cannot afford to be distracted. But arguably Ygritte is more compromised than Jon. She believes that, since both can trace their ancestry back to the First Men, the only difference between Free Folk and Northerners is where they were when the Wall went up. She's therefore less hostile to Jon than she appears and more willing to believe him than her comrades. She has three opportunities to kill him but her feelings for him make her miss or hesitate. The last time she aims for him she gets killed herself before she can kill him.

Jon joined Mance Rayder's band of Free Folk to infiltrate their camp and find out where and how they plan to attack the Wall. When Ygritte discovered that he has not really come round to their cause and is still a 'crow' at heart she should have killed him but still believed his feelings towards her would prove stronger than his oath. Jon's refusal to kill the old man at the windmill alerts the other members of the advance party to the fact that he would betray them and Ygritte has to be restrained from saving him from them. Later on she catches up with him as he drinks from a stream and has an opportunity to kill him. Again she cannot do it – although she puts three arrows in him none of them delivers a fatal blow. Ygritte is an expert shot and, as Tormund points out, had she meant to kill Jon she would have done it; if he's not dead it's because she didn't want him dead. Jon escapes and makes it home to Castle Black, in poor shape but alive, meaning that he is able to share the Free Folk's plans with his Night's Watch brothers. Ygritte spends most of the fourth season talking about wanting to kill Jon but when she finally has an opportunity he turns his puppy-dog eyes on her and once again she hesitates, this time fatefully as she is shot in the back by one of Jon's compatriots. For all her tough talk Ygritte is an idealist and a romantic; she dies wishing she and Jon could be back in the cave where she helped him break his Night's Watch oath.

It would be nice if we could compartmentalize our lives like that, if one relationship could be isolated from the others and have no effect on it but we know it's not like that. Our business lives and home lives have an effect on each other even if it's just in terms of work–life balance. The difficulties fall into two broad categories: involving people with whom you have a non-work relationship in your business, and sex in the workplace. The latter is potentially more damaging and clearly causes problems; just ask President Clinton. While you are not going to be hauled up in front of a senate committee or have your sexual practices broadcast to the world is it really a good idea to start a relationship at work? Some businesses are so aware of the problems caused by sex at work that they, like the Night's Watch, have an outright ban on relationships at work.

If you begin a relationship with somebody senior or junior to you in the business how might that affect both the business and the romantic relationship? Might you find yourself conforming to the same hierarchy in the relationship as at work? If you get a promotion can you really be sure it was solely based on your work? What if other people find out, how does it look then if you're sleeping with the boss? Going back to the Clinton affair, remember it wasn't just Bill who suffered. In fact, other than the obvious humiliations, Bill appeared to suffer relatively little – he got to remain part of the Clinton power couple and complete his term as president, and people still seem to love him. But an intern who has sex with the president – 'That Woman' must be an overambitious slut, right?

Before the affair was discovered Monica Lewinsky was headed for a great career – no matter what the press might have said about her at the time, they don't take any less than the best as White House interns. Since the discovery of the affair in 1998 she has had no career. She managed to trade off her notoriety for a while but found it difficult to get jobs in her chosen sector, marketing for non-profit organizations, because she was always recognized and only known for one thing. In fact one interviewer actually said that they would love to take her on but couldn't do it without a Letter of Indemnification from the Clintons; they were worried what it could mean for an organization that employed Monica Lewinsky in the event that Hilary Clinton became president.

It's also affected Lewinsky's relationships, as an article she wrote for *Vanity Fair* in June 2014 implies, her friends' lives having moved on to marriage and kids but hers having not. Men willing to take on the woman who nearly toppled a president, a political joke, are clearly not easy to find. As Lewinsky herself states in the article, 'In my early 20s, I was too young to understand the real-life consequences, and too young to see that I would be sacrificed for political expediency. I look back now, shake my head in disbelief, and wonder: what was I – what were we – thinking? I would give anything to go back and rewind the tape.'

You may not threaten the presidency or jeopardize the business by starting a relationship at work but your career will almost certainly suffer. By all means if after careful thought you think 'this could be the one' and it seems more important than your job at that company then follow your heart. But tread very carefully, keep your relationship at work entirely professional and if that's not possible then start looking for a new job.

4

BE DECISIVE – NO MATTER HOW TOUGH IT IS

Ned Stark: *"Do you understand why I had to kill him? … The man who passes the sentence should swing the sword."*

In the very first episode we learn the tough way a leader must dispense justice. Will, the only member of the Night's Watch scouting party to survive the wights flees the scene, forsaking his duties. Captured by the Starks, he is tried as a deserter, for which he is sentenced to death. As Ned Stark explains to his younger son, Bran, justice means that the man who gives the verdict also delivers the punishment. Despite the fact that Will attempts to make a case for his desertion and admits to his cowardice Lord Stark still goes ahead with the punishment; he swore an oath when he joined the Night's Watch and the law is the law. It's unlikely that you'll ever have to execute anybody, but leaders are often faced with tricky decisions – so how do you act decisively while retaining the hearts of your employees?

One of the hardest things any manager has to do is dismiss a member of the team. This could be for one of a number of reasons, the hardest of which is probably losing team members due to 'downsizing', where the business has to come first and the employee most likely has done nothing to deserve being let go. Regardless of the reasons for the dismissal there are a few things to bear in mind which will make the process easier on both you and the member of the team you are firing.

First off do your preparation. Make sure that you have the reasons for dismissal straight in your mind and you are fully aware of the process. This will protect you against any reprisals later on. It will also make it easier for you to stand firm in the face of a pleading employee if you've already been through all the arguments they might come up with against their dismissal. Nothing will make you look weaker to your company, the employee and your team if you take it this far and then fail to stick to your guns. Think of the bosses on *The Apprentice*; how would Lord Sugar or Donald Trump look if, after they delivered their 'You're fired' verdict, they allowed themselves to be swayed by the fired candidate? While approaching the moment with callous delivery and a pointing finger is inadvisable you can learn from their clear-cut statement.

And here's a secondary point; you have to be crystal clear. The last thing you want is for the person to leave the meeting not realizing what is happening to them because you can't bring yourself to say the words or to not understand the reason for their dismissal because you've tried to soften the blow by calling dismissal on grounds of unsuitability for the job a redundancy. White lies and vagueness can get you into hot water later on if the employee decides to contest their dismissal. It can also make the whole process worse for all involved and do your career no favours.

Theon shows us how not to go about delivering a fatal blow when, during the sack of Winterfell, in order to demonstrate his authority to his less-than-impressed Iron Islands soldiers, he is expected to execute Ser Rodrik Cassel. Theon's known him for years and was trained by Ser Rodrik in the art of combat. Clearly this is not something Theon wants to happen (let alone wants to do), but he realizes that if he does not carry out the punishment he'll lose the men completely. His lack of commitment to the punishment causes extra suffering for Ser Rodrik (there's a lot of hacking before his head is severed) and has the opposite effect on Theon's men than he'd hoped.

Second, do it yourself. If your boss has asked you to get rid of some of your team members then unfortunately it is you who has to do it, especially if you've been involved in the decision (and with any luck you will have been consulted). If the company has made the decision without you then you may have a case to argue against having to deliver the blow but it's unlikely you'll impress anybody with this kind of seemingly cowardly behaviour so if you're planning to make a career at this company you'll simply have to man (or woman) up and do the deed.

If you've seen the film *Up in the Air* you'll be aware of the existence of the corporate downsizer. This is a person hired by a large company to do the firing for them and is most commonly used in the case of mass redundancies. While this ensures that your message is delivered professionally be careful when using such a service. It makes it look like the company either doesn't care or is too cowardly to face the person who's being made redundant. It's possibly the most callous way to deliver your message and the impersonality of it, treating employees as items on a balance sheet rather than people, could make a bad situation worse. As the UK's Trades Union Congress, which represents more than six million union members, points out, involving an outside party could communicate a lack of responsibility towards workers and generate resentment.

Third, be as generous as you can. This may mean being financially generous in order to effect a swift severance, allowing the employee to work out a notice period that gives them a chance to find a job or simply allowing them to present their departure to colleagues in a way that enables them to save face. Don't forget that there is a certain amount of shame even in being made redundant, after all the fact that this person was asked to leave implies that they were less valuable to the company than somebody else who might also have been given the boot (a good example of a phrase not to use). Anything that avoids nastiness and wrangling now or awkwardness when you run across them in a future business scenario should be considered regardless of your personal feelings towards the team member you're dismissing.

Finally, remember the rest of the team. The departures will mean adjustments between the remaining members. The way the team works will have become shaped to fit in with the individual personalities involved and now the team make-up has changed that process will have to be gone through again. Expecting people just to carry on as if nothing has happened is unreasonable and, particularly if the person or people who left were popular, could lead to an unhappy or even uncooperative team. Pre-empt this by organizing a meeting or event where you acknowledge the changes and potential difficulties but also thank the team for pulling together and praise them for their abilities to get through this difficult time.

5

KEEP YOUR WORD

Jaime Lannister: *"So many vows. They make you swear and swear ... Defend the king, obey the king, obey your father, protect the innocent, defend the weak. But what if your father despises the king? What if the king massacres the innocent? It's too much. No matter what you do you're forsaking one vow or another."*

In order to secure troops and support in his ongoing battle against the Lannisters, King in the North, Robb Stark, has to promise to marry one of Walder Frey's daughters. Walder Frey's daughters are not renowned as great beauties. Talisa Maegyr, on the other hand, is both good looking and morally upright (when Robb first meets her she's tending wounded soldiers). Therefore Robb marries Talisa, in spite of all good sense and his mother's warning that crossing Walder Frey will be a mistake. In order to placate Walder, Robb's Uncle Edmure is promised to one of his daughters instead. But alliances have already been altered and plots have been hatched … Now we're not saying that any of your broken vows are going to lead to your head being replaced by that of a dire wolf but you'll certainly lose respect if you're seen not to keep your word.

As a wise fool once said, 'Fool me once, shame on … shame on you. Fool me … – you can't get fooled again.' Although he expressed it ineptly Dubya was right: once you've been seen to break your word most people will be far more wary in their dealings with you. For somebody so morally upright Robb is astonishingly casual in breaking the promise made to Lord Frey on his behalf. Perhaps he thinks the dishonourable Lord Frey is unworthy of being treated morally or perhaps, like his father and half-brother, his impulsiveness gets the better of him and he acts before he thinks through the situation properly. He certainly fails as a leader by putting his personal benefit before that of his family and supporters.

Other people take their oaths far more seriously. Many of them, like Arya with her kill-list, which she recites every night, make vengeful oaths, but Brienne is truly a woman of honour. Throughout her journey with Jaime she is driven on by her promise to Lady Stark that she will bring her daughters to safety. There were many occasions in the journey when it would have been easier for her simply to give Jaime up to the Northerners who wanted him dead but she battled on, even suffering near rape and a fight with a bear in trying to uphold her promise. Brienne is not one to choose ease or convenience over honour; having chosen to be a knight (although she could never formally become one) she stands by the chivalric principles of that role. To do otherwise would be unthinkable to her. When Jaime charges her with continuing her mission by finding Sansa Stark and keeping her safe from those who would have her executed for Joffrey's murder he presents her with a sword made out of the Valyrian steel of Ned Stark's weapon. He reminds her that the best swords have names, and Brienne solemnly decides to call hers 'Oathkeeper'.

We are not judged merely by what we say. Vowing to do something is the first part of any plan and it's easy to impress with promises but if you aren't seen to act on these promises you'll quickly lose the trust of employees, customers and stakeholders alike. The domestic energy market seems to be particularly prone to breaking promises – to customers, government and employees.

In the UK there is a regulator called Ofgem which checks that these energy companies are acting fairly towards the market. In recent years Ofgem has found that five of the six large energy suppliers in the UK broke promises to consumers by overstating the savings they would make by switching to them from the supplier they were with at the time. Put simply they promised that bills would be lower and they weren't; in fact in some cases customers actually found they were paying more with the new supplier. In December 2014 Ofgem also fined UK energy suppliers for failing to reach agreed environmental targets. The suppliers had committed to the government's Community Energy Savings Programme, under which energy suppliers were required to deliver fixed targets of energy saving measures to help lower carbon emissions and reduce bills for households in low income areas by 31 December 2012. When the suppliers failed to deliver on time several thousand households missed out on energy efficiency measures during the cold winter of 2012–13. One of the suppliers, British Gas, was fined £11.1 million; Ofgem found that senior management had failed to take 'appropriate action' to make sure the measures were delivered on time, nor did they do enough to respond to changes in market conditions or resolve delivery problems.

While £11.1 million is a relatively small amount to a massive energy company, every time there is a story like this it dents consumer confidence. It's little wonder that a recent survey by market researchers YouGov found that 56% of UK consumers felt that energy companies 'treat people with contempt'. Only 7% of people surveyed said they would 'trust the UK utilities industry to focus on the best interests of its customers and wider society', while 61% disagreed. A massive 42% agreed that 'energy supply companies have worse ethics than big businesses in other sectors', with only 13% disagreeing with the statement.

There's little energy consumers can do against massive suppliers of electricity and gas without the help of watchdogs and media – people have to light and heat their homes and there aren't many who'll be prepared to go back to log fires and candles in protest. It's probably because of this that this industry has been able to get away with so many broken promises in the past. But not all businesses have the security of supplying an essential product. If your organization failed to deliver on promises to your consumers what would that mean for the business? Or if you failed to deliver on an important project for your company what would that do for your career – would you be trusted with another project of that magnitude, given the pay rise you want or considered for promotion? It's simple – to stand any chance of career advancement or business success you have to be seen to deliver on your promises.

6

POWER IS GREATNESS

Varys: *"Power resides where men believe it resides; it is a trick, a shadow on the wall, and a very small man can cast a very large shadow."*

This was something the sixteenth-century Florentine politician Niccolo Machiavelli knew. It's something Robb Stark discovered too late to avoid his tragic fate. Of all the shocks *Game of Thrones* has delivered over its four seasons (and counting) the Red Wedding, which features in the episode 'The Rains of Castamere', was the most talked about. Even before you knew what happened you knew something big was going to take place. It more or less crashed the internet. Because of this it's unlikely that you'll need any recap of the events (and if you haven't seen it, stop reading now). Next time someone describes a drunken wedding to you as 'carnage', you'll have a handy visual reference.

But the internet-crashing shock wasn't fundamentally about death. There's loads of that on TV. What really made this stand out was that it broke the rules – the story just wasn't supposed to go this way. We'd invested in the revenge story of Robb Stark and his family who, in Hollywood narrative terms, should clearly win their war against the Lannisters because that's the way things are done in fairy stories. Therefore, when they get cut into small chunks at the Red Wedding, and fail epically as a result, it's not the way things should happen. Consider:

- Robb Stark's wise and (mostly) good father, who loved his kids so much that he even fathered an extra one while he was off having a war, was murdered by the Lannisters for political reasons. Therefore avenging him is a righteous quest.

- Lannisters are weaselly snivelling cheats who make Shakespeare's Richard III look like Nelson Mandela.

- The Starks have an attractive, macho, mud-caked integrity; they do not dress in silly foppish clothes or wear ridiculous little crowns. Again, not like the nasty Lannisters.

Many of the stories we read, watch and tell, the religions and beliefs we follow, the news we watch and therefore the assumptions we make are based on the idea that virtue gets a reward. We build these stories into a 'Great Man' (it's almost always a man) narrative, in which a few extraordinary people shape our destiny for the better. This was first expressed by the historian Thomas Carlyle in 1841, in his book *On Heroes, Hero-Worship, and The Heroic in History*, in which he wrote, 'The history of the world is but the biography of great men.'

Niccolo Machiavelli, writing more than 300 years before him, had a rather more nuanced appreciation of the Great Man. When he wrote *The Prince* as a leadership manual for medieval rulers, he knew two things: first, that it really helps to get stuff done if you are perceived as great. He was less fussy about actual greatness or virtue – perhaps because he'd spent a lot of time around the Medici and Borgia versions of the Great Man. The second thing, as Machiavelli warns us towards the end of his celebrated book, is that 'greatness' is fundamentally about happenstance: being the right person, in the right place, at the right time.

And so he undermined the Great Man Theory before Carlyle created it. But we look for a neater story, that great men are fulfilling a destiny. The Starks must win because they deserve it. Something they believe themselves. It also helps us to take orders if we believe that we follow people not just because they are powerful, but because they are better than us in some way.

Great Man Theory underpins the modern idea of the hero CEO too. There is an economic theory known as 'just desserts' (in the US, 'just deserts') which argues that the financial rewards of the additional value created by an innovation or business should flow to the person who created it. Greg Mankiw, one of the greatest economists alive today, recently wrote a paper on this called 'Defending the One Percent'. It's easy to read, and argues, for example, that innovators like Steve Jobs deserved their extraordinary rewards.

There are two arguments against this. First of all, Steve Jobs didn't design the products that Apple sells. Innovation is a team effort, involving thousands of deserving, hard-working people, some of whom get minimum wage.

Secondly, even if we think there might be a limited number of great men to reward, who exactly are they? Who gets the revenues from the iPhone? Is it the person who invented the iPhone, or the telephone, or the one who invented electricity, or who created outsourced manufacturing, or even the internet? Any one of them would have a legitimate claim on a piece of the action, and few of them profited anything like as much as Jobs. What Jobs did have was charisma and a belief in his own greatness – he was Apple.

Machiavelli knew that the necessary condition for becoming a Great Man isn't to possess greatness according to some moral or intellectual standard (it might help, but judging by the people in Mankiw's 1% it's clearly not essential). The perception of greatness comes from the power, not the other way around. People have to think you're going to win, or they won't give you a chance to prove it.

But the Red Wedding reminds us (as does much of *Game of Thrones*) that, while this is a necessary condition of greatness, it's not sufficient. You also have to actually win: history never even thinks about virtuous people without power, and soon forgets losers. So when our Great Man Theories are hacked to bits in front of our disbelieving eyes, it's uncomfortable. But it's a useful reminder of the sources and limits of power.

7

STICK TO THE TRUTH

Baelish: *"Is there someone in your service who you trust completely?"*
Ned: *"Yes."*
Baelish: *"The wiser answer would have been 'No', my Lord."*

From very early in the story Jorah Mormont is at Daenerys' side advising her, but where did he come from and why is he in Essos? He manages to get very close to her purely by seeming to have her best interests at heart. In fact he was originally sent by Varys to spy on her in order to earn a pardon for slave trading. Captivated by her personality, he realizes she really could become Queen of Westeros, so saves her from being poisoned. By the time Daenerys discovers the truth about Jorah she has come to rely on his counsel and trust his decisions so getting rid of him is unbearably tough for both of them.

The good thing about Tyrion's hired bodyguard Bronn is that he is a sellsword, a mercenary. His motives are not confused and he has no loyalty. As he explains to Tyrion early on, as long as Tyrion has money to pay him he can count on him. He's not his sworn sword or his friend, nor is he honourable. But unlike Jorah Mormont he doesn't pretend to be – he's completely honest. When it comes down to deciding whether to be Tyrion's Champion and take on the Mountain in trial by combat there's no question of him helping Tyrion out. Cersei has offered him a bride set to inherit lands as a bribe for not representing Tyrion, and going up against the Mountain would in any case amount to suicide. When he apologizes Tyrion simply says, "Why are you sorry? Because you're an evil bastard with no conscience and no heart? That's what I liked about you in the first place." Tyrion's not really angry or let down because much as he might have hoped that Bronn would be his champion he never expected it.

So who would you prefer to have on your team: a heartless bastard who you know is a heartless bastard or a man who you can't be sure you know at all?

From an employment perspective you might really want that job. Perhaps you think you can do the job but don't have all the qualifications or experience required. So why not embellish your resumé? Well it's a huge risk – and as with all risks you have to balance the rewards against the potential dire consequences. Yes, your secret may remain safe. It might be uncovered but because you're doing the job well you get to keep it. The more likely consequence of discovery is that you lose both the job and your reputation. At any level in the business a company is going to find it hard to work with somebody they are unsure they can trust. If you are in a more senior position there's a PR nightmare for the company too – it's going to make it very difficult for an organization to look trustworthy if it employs known liars. Daenerys gets rid of Jorah because she's insulted, scared and would look weak and foolhardy were she to keep him in her employ after the revelations of his original reasons for getting close to her.

According to First Advantage, a firm whose services include resumé checks for employers, roughly 25% of resumés contain some kind of fabrication. Some are not particularly serious and may even be accidental but around a third are big lies. According to the firm, the most common things to lie about are exam results, professional qualifications, past duties and employment dates (for example to cover up a career break that might lead to awkward questions). The point of a resumé is to present you in a positive light so it's easy to fall into the fabrication trap, but most career experts would counsel against it.

Scott Thompson discovered the perils of lying when he was appointed as CEO of Yahoo in January 2012. In his resumé he stated that he had degrees in both accounting and computer science. Daniel S. Loeb, manager of a hedgefund with shares in Yahoo took it upon himself to check up on Thompson and discovered that while he did have an accounting degree there was no evidence that he had one in computer science. He wrote that if the credentials did turn out to be falsified it would both undermine Thompson's credibility as a technology expert and reflect poorly on his character. Yahoo was going through a tough period and needed a trustworthy CEO then more than ever. Although initially supportive of Thompson, Yahoo did its own investigation. Thompson resigned from the company in May 2012. He did walk away with a considerable amount of money but he's now on public record as having lied to his employer. His career prospects have been severely damaged. Once the truth was obvious Thompson claimed that the error had been introduced many years ago by a headhunting firm he'd worked with. But when the agency in question was able to produce the resumé Thompson originally submitted to them it became clear that this was another lie. This is another dangerous thing about lying – one lie often requires another to back it up. Keeping up with all those untruths can get very demanding.

Once you gain a senior role that resumé becomes a profile and your lie is out in front of the whole world for ever more. This was a problem encountered by former president of the US Olympic Committee, Sandra Baldwin. She claimed to have an undergraduate degree from the University of Colorado and a doctorate from Arizona State but a reporter researching an article on her for the University of Colorado Alumni magazine discovered this wasn't the case – her undergraduate degree was from ASU and she had no qualifications at all from Colorado. Commenting on the lies on her resumé Baldwin admitted, 'I should have changed it a long time ago, but once it was published, it got paralyzing. Now I'm going to have to live with it for the rest of my life.'

If job hunters need to tell the truth employers need to learn to do proper background checks. Yahoo and the US Olympic Committee need only have undertaken a few simple investigations and they would have avoided a lot of embarassment. If you can't afford the services of a company like First Advantage do a little of your own digging. For example it is relatively simple to check qualifications with the institution they were allegedly obtained from and make sure you take up references with past employers. Yes, you are legally entitled to fire somebody if you later discover they lied on their CV but it will be a whole lot easier not to employ them in the first place.

8

BE CROSS-CULTURALLY SAVVY

Daenerys: *"Ser Jorah, I don't know how to say 'thank you' in Dothraki."*
Jorah: *"There is no word for 'thank you' in Dothraki."*

When Daenerys Targaryen's brother Viserys forces her into a strategically advantageous marriage by selling her to Dothraki leader Khal Drogo in exchange for troops, she's rather less than happy. But she makes an effort to understand the customs of the Dothraki and learn their language. By so doing she manages to win round her husband and the Dothraki so that even after Drogo's untimely death many are willing to follow her as their khaleesi, their queen. Drogo for his part makes no attempt to learn Daenerys' customs or language; when she asks on their wedding night if he knows the common tongue he simply says "No". In fact that's his answer to all her questions including, "Is 'No' the only word you know?" So it's clear that she is going to have to make all the effort, although perhaps that's only fair since they are in his country enjoying his hospitality.

Dothraki customs are not easy to take if you've been brought up in a relatively civilized place. The wedding celebrations seem to involve ritualized rape and murder – as Illyrio Mopatis points out, "A Dothraki wedding without at least three deaths is considered a dull affair." They are also superstitious and when Daenerys is found to be pregnant she has to eat a stallion's heart in order to enable them to prophesy whether the baby will be a boy. Because of their supposed savagery Viserys is both disgusted by and incredibly dismissive of them and thinks he can play them. He always maintains that he is superior to them (a bit rich coming from somebody whose family practises incest in order to keep their line pure) and when he is advised that they will go to war for him only if the omens favour war he shouts, "I piss on Dothraki omens." Such failure to ingratiate himself with his hosts, people he needs in order to further his cause, does his ambitions no favours and leads to his eventual gruesome demise.

Unless you're very unlucky you're unlikely to have to bridge such a vast cultural chasm or blunder so gravely if you do, but it is likely if you deal with suppliers, collaborators or customers in other parts of the world, if your company merges with a foreign company or if you employ people from other countries that you will experience culture shocks. Cultures vary in their approaches to many things from the way they make decisions, to the line between business and personal relationships, to their treatment of women – even in their relationship with time.

For example Americans are very individualistic and see the world in terms of personal achievement, whereas in China the focus is on the group; what seems like initiative to an American might look like selfish behaviour to somebody from the Far East. Communication is one of the first difficulties you will encounter – a straight-talking German is going to seem very rude to somebody from Japan, while the German might well be frustrated by her Japanese colleague's seeming inability to say what he means, since that culture prefers indirect communication. These are just two examples in what can at times seem like a minefield of cultural stumbling blocks. If you're not prepared for these differences it can lead to confusion and crossed wires, you may offend your business partners or be offended yourself and you might even lose business for your company. So the simplest and best piece of advice is to research thoroughly any new culture where you're about to do business. The second is to learn to compromise.

If you're unprepared to compromise on how business is done and insist that everybody conforms to your culture you're going to find your cross-cultural journey very difficult. Cross-cultural management consultants Trompenaars Hampden-Turner talk about this process of cultural negotiation and understanding as 'reconciling dilemmas'. Companies that can reconcile dilemmas will be the most successful. Cultural compromise is particularly difficult for English-speaking nations, which are so used to people speaking their language they don't even appreciate that there are cultural differences until they come up against a blockage. If you're from a country such as the USA that has become used to dominating the world, not just politically but in terms of business and culture, the first time you encounter a different way of understanding and moving through the world it can be a real shock. This was central to Viserys' downfall. He grew up believing his family was meant to rule the world and feeling entitled to expect people to do his bidding. Even after his father, King Aerys II, was murdered and he and his sister were exiled he continued to think of his family and himself as superior to everybody else. His failure to get his head round his changed circumstances meant that he was unable to adjust his behaviour and ultimately meant that he failed in his quest to become king.

You're missing a trick though if you think of cultural difference as a 'problem'. The ease of global travel as well as technologies that make it possible to do business across thousands of miles without leaving your desk mean that the opportunities for those who are equipped to do business around the world are now greater than they ever were. If you take the time to understand how other cultures expect to do business and then try to fit together your different working methodologies in a way that is mutually acceptable the potential rewards are great. As cross-cultural management experts Debby Swallow and Eilidh Milnes point out, 'organizations that align their people and their culture by creating a sense of relatedness and belonging, team spirit and mutual trust, outperform those that don't.'

9

NETWORK, NETWORK, NETWORK

Varys:*"Knowledge is my trade, my lady ... My little birds are everywhere."*

In a world where trust is in short supply the most influential people keep their ears to the ground. Lord Varys, Petyr Baelish and Cersei Lannister all run networks of spies in King's Landing. They play their own cards close to their chests and tease out the secrets of others. While we don't advocate taking ownership of a brothel in order to learn what your colleagues and rivals are up to it does pay to have regular meetings in more relaxed circumstances where people feel more able to be open and talk about their plans – work opportunites are more readily discovered this way than through official channels.

In an early episode of the first series Baelish walks around the palace gardens with Ned Stark. He counsels him to be cautious what he says here, pointing out that a certain child is one of Varys's spies, a gardener spies for Cersei and a pious-looking Septa is one of his own. He, Cersei and Varys all recognize the value of connections and information. Varys is so well-connected throughout both Westeros and Essos that he is nicknamed the Spider, alluding to his intricately constructed web of informants. Varys and Baelish are both pragmatists who have allegiance only to themselves, meaning that they're never morally compromised or hampered by commitment to a particular cause. Their methods and agents are clearly known to other players of this particular game but most other people are unaware that there is so much spying going on, giving the three players a huge advantage over rivals.

It's through working their connections and using the information they obtain that both Varys and Baelish have risen from relatively humble origins – Varys was born a slave – to their current influential positions on the small council. The two may not like each other but, knowing a worthy opponent when they see one, respect one another. Their ambitions are not the same but clearly at some point one may feel the need to get rid of the other. In a hostile environment such as this it's critical to be well-connected, to be able to call in favours and count on relationships with other nobles that will ensure they rally to your cause rather than that of the other guy. What you don't want to do is find yourself in the position of requiring a favour from an untrustworthy lord like Walder Frey, whose idea of networking is to offer a series of daughters up for marriage. Though even being married to a daughter of his might not make you more likely to gain the allegiance of somebody this slippery, as Catelyn Stark cautions, "some men take their oaths more seriously than others".

Unless you're incredibly unlucky you won't find yourself in a business environment as tense and hostile as the War of the Five Kings, nor should you need to act as cynically as the *Game of Thrones* networkers but (as no doubt you've been told many times) networking is still a crucial activity if you want to get ahead. It's also a commonly misunderstood activity, with many people either believing handing out business cards and having a profile on LinkedIn will suffice, or only thinking of networking when they have something to sell or are looking for a new job. Like waiting until you need to cross the Trident at the Twins to negotiate with Walder Frey, networking only when you want something is going to be fraught with difficulty. Yes, you're short of time and days are long enough without starting them with a breakfast networking meeting but if you value your career, want to sell your services or make a success of your business you're going to have to constantly work on your business relationships.

Some people are also put off by the perceived phoneyness of these events – shouldn't the whole process be more organic? Well yes, it can be, after all if you approach it in the right way anything from your Italian class to chatting after your Wednesday night football kick about to your cup of tea after choir practice can lead to a work opportunity. The good thing about the formal meetings is that people are guaranteed to be receptive – you've all come along with the same thing in mind. It's rather like the difference between trying to chat somebody up at a party and looking for the love of your life on a speed-dating night. Whatever works best for you.

If you do go for a formal networking meeting don't be put off if the first one you attend isn't a success; some are better than others or simply more suitable for you, so be prepared to attend a few before you find one that fits. Remember too that you need to do your homework; think about why you're there, the kind of connections you're hoping to make and why people should want to speak to you. Most importantly, remember to begin with that these people are strangers and at first they will just want to get to know you. Too many people make the mistake of expecting to turn up at an event and sell to strangers. That's like expecting to sleep with somebody after your first speed-dating encounter with them – its unlikely to happen and extremely inadvisable. Bestselling author and networking guru Ivan Misner is founder of the world's largest business networking organization, BNI. He points out that when you first join a networking group you need to avoid the urge to sell and remember, 'You have to earn the loyalty and engagement of your referral sources. Your current goal has two parts: (1) to meet the right people, and (2) to develop deep relationships with them over time.' Impatience will get you nowhere; you really do have to play the long game when it comes to networking. Oh, and definitely no hopping into bed with your fellow networkers.

10

IF YOU CAN'T LEAD, INFLUENCE

Varys: *"Influence grows like a weed. I tended mine patiently until its tendrils reached from the Red Keep all the way across to the far side of the world."*

Being a woman in the *Game of Thrones* world sucks. If you're low-born you're a servant or a prostitute and if you're high-born it's more or less the same thing but with nicer clothes. Women are there to cement alliances by being married off, and to produce heirs. Other than that their lot is just listening to their husbands spout off, doing needlework and talking to other women about needlework. Hardly surprising then that Cersei Lannister, every bit as intelligent as her brothers, is bored, and pretty angry about her lot. She therefore spends a lot of her time plotting, and pulling strings behind the scenes. You may not be the leader – yet – but you can still see some of your plans come to fruition if you know what to say to whom.

First as queen and then as queen regent Cersei has immense influence and uses it to play events to her liking. Robert is considerably more pliable than Joffrey (teenagers, eh). Her technique with him is to be respectful and deferential while subtly suggesting exactly what he should do. When the leadership of the Night's Watch see the coming winter and their vulnerability in the face of it and whatever horrors it may bring – they are a bunch of "undisciplined boys and tired old men" and number fewer than a thousand – they ask Tyrion to put their case to Cersei so that she may influence the king to help them out (she doesn't). It's unclear whether this is because they know that Cersei is a skilled influencer or whether that's just what's expected of the queen. After all women have been influencing men – and getting blamed for their bad decisions – ever since Eve suggested to Adam he might want to think about eating more fruit.

It's hard to like Cersei or any of the most skilled influencers in *Game of Thrones*; they usually use their gifts for ill and to plot the overthrow or demise of more sympathetic characters. Cersei gets Tyrion arrested for the murder of Joffrey even though she probably doesn't really think he killed him, and Petyr Baelish uses the hold he has over Lyana to get Jon Arryn killed – the event that sparked off the whole bloody war. But both are very successful in getting what they want so perhaps we can learn something about influencing for good from their examples.

In the first instance, when Cersei convinces people that Tyrion should be arrested it's all about timing. She's been waiting to get rid of him ever since they were children, blaming him for killing their mother, who died giving birth to him, so is glad to seize the opportunity. The Kingsguard, who failed to prevent Joffrey's murder, will be keen to act so it's easy to influence them to seize Tyrion. Tywin will be keen to see that order is restored as swiftly as possible and were he to delay arresting Tyrion he might make himself look weak and indecisive so he too is easy to influence in this matter. But had Cersei not accused Tyrion it is unlikely that he would have been arrested at all.

So how do you pick your moment if you want to influence your manager? Say, for example, you want him to give you the lead on a particularly prestigious project. First of all make sure you choose the right moment to ask him. You need to catch him when he's relaxed and has time to think, not as he's rushing between meetings or busy trying to sort out some crisis (unless you have an audacious plan to catch him off guard). You also need to be sure that he's disposed favourably towards you – perhaps you've recently impressed him in a meeting, made a great hire or saved the company some money.

Petyr Baelish is adept at stating things in his influencee's language. He makes sure he approaches Lyana in a way that she wants him to. She's always been in love with him so, distasteful as it is to him, he approaches her as a lover, swallowing his feelings for the sake of his ambition. When he later gets her to write to her sister saying that she's fled King's Landing in fear of her life because she believes that Jon was poisoned by the Lannisters it's too easy really. He knows that this is a message that the Starks will readily fall for as it fits in with their beliefs regarding the corruption of the Lannisters.

If you want to influence somebody a good way of doing it is to follow Petyr's lead and speak their language, to see things from their point of view and communicate what you want to them in terms that they will find easy to understand. So back to that project you want the lead on, think about what your boss wants not what you want. He's not interested that you feel this is the challenge you've been waiting for, nor does he care that you'll get a sense of achievement from doing it. What he wants to know is how it will elevate the company's profile and hence his standing within it. So talk about the business (not too presumptiously now), the project and (without looking like a kiss-ass) what the successful completion of said project will do for him.

Lastly be specific – all the great timing and empathy in the world won't work if you haven't made it clear what you want from the person you're influencing. Tyrion manages to mess up his communication with Shae twice; first by being indirect in his request and second by lying. He realizes that Cersei has found out about Shae and it is no longer safe for her to remain in King's Landing. He therefore sends Varys to persuade her to leave for Pentos, by pointing out that her presence in the city endangers Tyrion, and give her enough money to set herself up nicely in a new location. But because Tyrion approaches her through a third party she feels as if she's being sidelined and treated as a whore, so angrily rejects the offer. So Tyrion tries another tack, this time telling her that he never loved her and always thought of her as a whore, in order to make her leave out of anger. This backfires when she is intercepted by Cersei (we presume) and persuaded to testify against Tyrion at his trial. Had Tyrion felt able to play it straight with Shae things might have gone better; instead by wishing to protect her – first by subtly trying to get her to leave and second by trying to make her hate him – he created confusion and misunderstanding that eventually led to tragedy. So when you leave the meeting with your boss make sure he is absolutely clear that you want to head up that prestigious project.

11

KEEP AN EYE ON THE FINANCES

Tycho Nestoris: *"Across the Narrow Sea your books are filled with words like 'usurper' and 'madman' and 'blood-right'. Here our books are filled with numbers. We prefer the stories they tell. More plain, less ... open to interpretation."*

War is expensive. The Lannisters came to prominence because they were rich and when Robert Baratheon became king he needed their money. He therefore married Cersei Lannister to get access to that money, which put her father, Tywin, in a powerful position. Now the Lannisters, after having to fend off attempts on the throne by Robb Stark and both Baratheon brothers, are themselves running out of money and have had to forge a similar alliance with the Tyrells. Stannis Baratheon, in a brilliantly prosaic move, has had to borrow money from the Iron Bank of Braavos.

When Ned Stark joins the small council as the Hand of the King, the master of coin, Petyr Baelish, informs him that the realm is already six million gold dragons in debt, and half of this is owed to the Lannister family. And that's before they all start slaughtering each other. Now it's hard to find the current exchange rate for gold dragons but we're guessing this isn't the kind of debt you can pay off by selling a few unwanted items from your attic on eBay. Baelish understands the importance of Tywin's money. He's scandalized when Ned proposes calling Tywin Lannister to court to answer for the crimes of his bannerman Gregor Clegane, who has been carrying out raids in the Riverlands. Pissing off the richest man in Westeros, when times are already tight seems foolhardy at best; there's a potential threat to the throne from across the sea (the Targaryens) and "it's gold that wins wars, not armies".

However, you need to be careful how you come by that gold. Across the sea Jorah counsels Daenerys against accepting financial aid. She's in a hurry to get over to Westeros and reclaim the throne but he thinks they should return quietly and drum up support over there rather than attacking from Essos with borrowed money and starting her reign in debt. Similarly, when Tyrion is appointed as Master of Coin and uncovers evidence that Baelish, the previous holder of the position, has overborrowed and put the crown heavily in debt, he worries about repaying the Iron Bank. This bank will not only refuse further loans when you fail to repay (as would your bank), but will also finance rebellions against you. This is exactly how Davos Seaworth persuades the bank to give Stannis a loan. He points out that the only reliable Lannister is Tywin, who is 67, and asks what will happen to the kingdom when he dies: none of his children or grandchildren seem like solid financial prospects.

If you don't keep on top of your finances you've no hope of winning the game of thrones and it's no different in real life. There's no escaping it, a good leader must know her company finances. If the shit hits the fan and you try to use ignorance as an excuse you'll just appear incompetent. In an article in *Entrepreneur* magazine, business consultant Peri Pakroo points out that a fear of or reluctance to deal with the finances is something she frequently encounters among owners of small- to medium-sized businesses. She notes that while hiring a bookkeeper or accountant to deal with the day-to-day financial tasks can help, it shouldn't be used as an excuse to completely take your eye off the finances. She says, 'If you merely keep up with the basics, you might avoid true financial disaster. But you'll definitely miss opportunities to thrive if you don't use your data to make strategic decisions.' If you neglect the numbers your business will pay the price.

It's not just smaller businesses that can fall foul of the finances though. In September 2014 £2 billion was wiped off the value of Britain's largest supermarket chain, Tesco, when it was revealed that an accounting error had overstated the projected profit of the company for the first six months of the year by more than £263 million ($421 million). The error seemed to stem from wrongly accounting when revenue from promotions would be received as well as glossing over the true extent of business costs such as money lost through out of date stock and stock theft. Basically, some very large numbers got put in the wrong column, making the half-year in question look more profitable. The four directors closest to the error were suspended immediately pending an investigation by the financial conduct authority, which has the power to prosecute companies that intentionally or recklessly mislead the Stock Exchange. Later on, payouts to the former CFO and Chief Executive, who both left shortly before the error came to light, were also suspended. Tesco was actually without a CFO at the time; the previous one having resigned in April with the new guy unable to start until November (due to a required period of gardening leave after leaving rival retailer Marks and Spencer). At the time the error was uncovered some City analysts called for the chairman, Sir Richard Broadbent to leave the company, pointing out that in presiding over such a huge error he had made his position untenable. Sir Richard for his part claimed to be part of the solution not part of the problem, stating gnomically that 'Things are always unnoticed until they are noticed.' A month later, after Tesco reported a 92% decline in pre-tax profits for the first half of 2014, he resigned.

When you're at the helm financial issues are always your responsibility, so it's essential that you make an effort to understand and take an interest in the company finances. No matter what size the business is or your role in it you will be at a disadvantage if you turn a blind eye to the numbers – they, more than any business plan, mission statement or polished web site tell the story of the business. Getting to grips with these stories will set you apart from less financially savvy colleagues.

12

THE PERILS OF CORPORATE INBREEDING

Petyr Baelish: *"Sometimes, I've heard, even brothers and sisters develop certain affections. And when those affections become common knowledge, well that is an awkward situation indeed, especially in a prominent family."*

'Alongside kinslaying and the violation of guest right, incest is proscribed by every major religion in Westeros,' the *Game of Thrones* Wiki tells us, 'Children born of incest are deemed abominations.' Didn't stop them doing it though. Clearly there's 'proscribed by every major religion' and 'who are you to tell us what to do?' The Targaryens were particularly keen on incest, interbreeding in order to keep their bloodline pure. King Aerys II Targaryen (the Mad King) married his own sister, Queen

Rhaella Targaryen. King Aerys made good on his nickname by going insane thanks to inbreeding, and his son Viserys didn't appear to be all there either.

This, you might conclude, would be an argument against imitating his actions. But Queen Cersei and her brother Jaime Lannister have, even by the beginning of the first series of *Game of Thrones*, been going at it for years. This has the unfortunate consequence that they produce barmy King Joffrey, a sort of psychotic Milky Bar Kid.

This is a pretty accurate depiction of the sexual behaviour of European royalty through several centuries. For example, John V of Armagnac in the fifteenth century took up with a young girl called Isabelle who was considered one of the greatest beauties in France. This was controversial because there had been talk of marrying her to Henry VI of England before he stepped in. It was even more controversial because she was also his sister. After they had two children John V promised to keep his codpiece buttoned while his sister was around, so the kerfuffle didn't exactly die down when they got married (claiming the Pope had told them it was OK), and had a third child.

The literal aristocrats of incestual ick were undoubtedly the Habsburgs, who bred so enthusiastically with their cousins that, by the seventeenth century, King Charles II was 'physically disabled, mentally retarded and disfigured'. Academic studies calculate that Habsburg marriages had up to 25% of genes in common (which would equate to having one grandparent in common).

You don't have to be a disciple of Sigmund Freud to be aware that incest fantasies are common; apparently every internet porno site has an incest category. But the Habsburgs weren't being kinky. Royal incest is about power. It keeps the fortune in the family – if your extended family is also in charge of the country next-door, then a political alliance means a family wedding, whether you are into that sort of thing or not.

So, if we concentrate on the sex, we're missing the point. This is about power, and keeping power close. Power influences the way the cake is cut: the more you concentrate power, the more of the cake you keep. What psychologists call 'other-regarding behaviour' is more common among those genetically closer to us, or those with a similar world view.

It often isn't a plan, but an outcome of a natural (though misguided) thought process, in which we trust and value people who look and talk like us. People in power share power with their 'family'. Few discriminate consciously, but only a small group of the population has the social capital (confidence, education, powerful friends and common experiences) to be part of the 'in group'. Are these always the best people to wield power? Your opinion may be influenced by whether you are in that group or not.

We assume that shareholder capitalism places controls on CEOs and their executive officers, just as royal alliances between families were meant to moderate the behaviour of each ruler: but when the powerful actors are 'family', the opposite can often be the case.

A recent survey at Muckety.com, a site that maps connections of the rich, famous and influential, showed how corporate dynasties intermarry by sitting on each other's boards, with 258 people serving on three boards and six serving on five boards. One result: a small group effectively decides one another's compensation, and we all know how executive pay has ballooned in the last thirty years at a far greater rate than profits have increased. That's not criminal. But scandals at Enron, WorldCom and many others – in which the performance of a supine board has been shown to be a contributing factor – shows what can happen when intermarriage gives too much power, with too little oversight, to the King Joffreys of the corporate world.

But it's not just massive corporations that can suffer from inbreeding. While you need to work with like-minded people, sometimes too much concurrence can lead to creative stagnation. Your reliable, hard working, committed team members may not always be an asset – if you and your team are in complete agreement about the direction you need to follow you may completely miss the ideas that could take you down exciting new avenues. Next time you need to toss around ideas for a new project how about inviting a few new people into the discussion – maybe from other departments or as consultants – just to gain a fresh perspective. If you're diplomatic and do it in such a way that nobody feels their nose is being pushed out you may find this freshens up your team thinking and gets everybody energized for the project in hand.

13

DON'T LET IT GO TO YOUR HEAD

Joffrey: *"I am the king! I will punish you!"*
Tywin: *"Any man who must say, 'I am the king' is no true king. I'll make sure you understand that when I've won your war for you."*

Game of Thrones has more than its fair share of nutcases. Lunacy seems to be rife among the upper echelons of society – hardly surprising given the continuous power struggles and the popularity of inbreeding. Daenerys Targaryen's father Aerys II Targaryen was known as the Mad King and King Joffrey is more than a little unstable. Life at the top of the ladder is precarious and constantly demanding so it shouldn't come as a shock to discover that not everybody is equipped to deal with it.

Robert Baratheon finds ruling far harder than winning the war. Winning is perhaps not all it's cracked up to be. He moans to

Ned that because of the war they never had the chance to be young, and talking to Barristan Selmy about the first man he killed he growls his frustrations noting that had that man lived: "today his wife would be making him miserable, his sons would be ingrates and he'd be waking three times in the night to piss into a bowl".

Ruling certainly took its toll on the Targaryens. As Cersei notes, "Half of the Targaryens went mad, didn't they? What's the saying? 'Every time a Targaryen is born the gods flip a coin.'" Judging by the names (Aerys the Mad King, Maegor the Cruel) 300 years of rule can really get to you. This is something that the last remaining Targaryen (under the age of 100) begins to realize as she learns more about the realities of being a queen.

Daenerys finds that freeing slaves and defeating their masters is easier than maintaining that victory or ruling. Once she has freed the people of Meereen she learns that since she left Astapor and Yunkai both have become corrupted again. She has to send Daario Naharis back to Yunkai to threaten the masters with the same fate as that of their Meereen counterparts if they don't stop the backsliding. Meanwhile in Meereen she finds that her court is filled with people needing her help in various matters and she also learns the consequences of some of her decisions.

A young man wants to bury his father with dignity but this man was one of the masters she had crucified in retribution for the crucifixion of the children. Another freed slave finds that he doesn't know what to do with his life now he's free. He's homeless and has no way of supporting himself. He begs to be allowed to sell himself back to his former owner. And she learns that one of her dragons has killed a child, forcing her to take action by locking the dragons in a catacomb where they can do no harm. As a leader you're constantly faced with decisions and there always seems to be more work than you can fit into a normal work day. It's hardly surprising then that many bosses feel the need to make their work days longer.

Harriet Green, the ex-boss of travel firm Thomas Cook, was known to sleep as little as three hours a night, get up for a 5am session in the gym, fire off some emails on the way to work and arrive in the office at quarter past seven. Clearly she was a busy woman; the company had found it difficult to cope with changes in the travel market and Green was the one who brought it back from the brink of disaster. But perhaps there was more to her habits than this. Once you're at the top you feel pressure to justify your position so you need to show those below you and your competitors that you're bigger and stronger than they are, a force to be reckoned with. Silverback gorillas do this by beating their chests, the Targaryens did it by forging a throne from the swords of their enemies and high-powered executives do it by proving they can get by on half the sleep mere mortals require and still do everything better than them. British prime minister Margaret Thatcher also got by on very little sleep (four hours apparently) and even after she'd resigned, her power plays continued to assert themselves. John Major, who followed her as prime minister, prefered the normal eight hours and found it impossible to maintain her pace.

Given the pressures of leadership it can be tempting to start devoting even more time to your work at the expense of the rest of your life. This is not necessarily harmful; if you love your job and nobody else (husband, kids, goldfish) is suffering because of the increased length of your absences from home by all means go ahead. But is it really necessary to forsake basics like sleep if you want to reach the top and stay there? Is it even healthy? In 2014 a group of British scientists warned that ignoring your body's sleep requirements can lead to serious illnesses. In particular, studies have shown the activity of DNA can be disrupted by short sleep durations. Dr Simon Archer, who conducted a study at the University of Surrey, explained that because of this, regularly sleeping too little or having disrupted sleep patterns can be linked to cardiovascular disease, diabetes, obesity and potentially cancer. On a more basic level work you do when tired is likely to be of a lower quality than what you do when you're fresh and alert.

Yes, there are some super-humans who can leap out of bed at 5am every day, refreshed after four hours of sleep but most of us need more; there's no point in being at the top if it's making you depressed and ill. Instead of working crazy hours to assert your superiority or to make sure everything gets done you need to find ways to work smart. Take time to work out why you need to spend so many extra hours at work and then figure out ways to improve the situation.

Once in charge you get to make the rules so make them work for you. For example, if you find interruptions are the bane of your life and that you're only able to get down to the main task of the day once everybody else has left, let it be known that people can only interrupt you at certain times or (if you're really important) only by appointment. Don't let email run your life either. Discipline yourself to only look at it at certain times of the day and try setting up some filters so only the really important stuff pops up in your main in box. Employ wisely and you'll be able to delegate tasks to your lieutenants rather than feeling like you have to do everything yourself.

Most of us do have to make some effort to maintain a work–life balance. It's great to be passionate, even to get carried away with the work you're doing but be careful not to get obsessed and stressed to the point that your managers, co-workers and reports start whispering behind your back that it's all too much for you. Workaholism can affect your health and relationships and may even work against your career in the long run.

14

PLAN FOR TOUGH TIMES

Maester Aemon: *"The Starks are always right eventually; winter is coming. This one will be long and dark things will come with it ... When winter does come, gods help us all if we're not ready!"*

The seasons in *Game of Thrones* are a little wacky. Regular 365-day years with a full range of seasons don't seem to happen, instead they have seasons of unpredictable and irregular length, meaning that while they can get long summers, they can also have very long winters. Many of the young people have only known summer (it's lasted nine years according to Maester Aemon); and they've also only known peace. But older folk remember a time when winter lasted a generation; Old Nan, who watches over Bran after his accident, tells him a story of the long night when children were born and lived and died without seeing the sun. At the start of season two Lord Baelish warns the small council that they have insufficient food for a winter lasting longer than five years, so if another long winter is on the horizon there are going to be some very tough times ahead.

The motto of House Stark, 'Winter is coming', has a dour, northern ring to it. Even in the midst of summer this family assumes something bad is just round the corner. Clearly the motto is applicable to more than just the weather. While the Stark approach to life is not going to make them the best folks to sit next to at a dinner party it has value, as long as they act on their beliefs rather than just gloomily spouting dire warnings. But while the Stark seat of Winterfell seems to be well equipped for colder months – it was built above hot springs which heat it even in the worst winters – its residents may not have been the best at planning ahead. In fact they seem pretty hopeless at directing the action, always instead having to react to the plots of others. So while Tywin Lannister is constantly working towards the advancement of his family, the Starks have preferred to keep themselves safely tucked away in their northern stronghold. When they are forced to act, through Baelish's carefully orchestrated murder of Jon Arryn and the seeds of suspicion he sows in Stark minds, they are already on the back foot. As the new Hand of the King, Ned is forced to travel to King's Landing, a place where he has cultivated no relationships and where he is therefore weak when he tries to face off against the well-connected Lannisters.

Wise leaders don't assume it'll always be summer for their business; they make sure they use the times of plenty to help bolster their resources for the almost inevitable tougher times ahead, and they always have a Plan B. In fact they engage in something called 'scenario planning'. Businesses that do this develop their strategies in line with external and unplannable events. In other words they set up some likely 'what if ...' scenarios and then devise strategies to cope with them. Obviously we're talking about well-researched likelihoods here, so while no sane business is going to worry about how it would cope in the event of an alien invasion, a forward-thinking, well-informed organization should devote some resources to things like looking at the way its industry is heading, assessing how government legislation might affect the business and watching the markets for worrying changes that might indicate a wintry recession. Working out what might occur is clearly just the first step. Once that has been done strategies can be developed and the way they might play out in the event of various scenarios can be assessed.

It can be tempting for businesses to just focus on one potential future and then put all their energies into working towards that future. Clearly this is a gamble. Yes, the returns could be very high if a business bets on the right future but equally large losses can be suffered by the business that bets on the wrong one. It's therefore important to get a clear idea of a range of possibilities. One way of predicting the future is to look to the past. It's something we all do, unconsciously and informally, when we try to make decisions in our careers, our businesses and our lives. Futurists have formalized this simple technique by collecting data from the past and creating systems to look for patterns within it. Once a pattern has been discerned it can be used to predict likely futures. There is still an element of uncertainty but it can be greatly reduced by using this method.

Scenario planning can be employed as part of a SWOT analysis. In this a company analyses its strengths and weaknesses and assesses the opportunities and threats that exist for it in the context of the scenarios it has identified. Depending on the attitude to risk of the organization in question it may choose simply to reduce its weaknesses in the face of threats or, conversely, might seek to increase its strengths to take advantage of the opportunities available. Most companies will attempt a combination of minimizing weaknesses and maximizing strengths.

Scenario planning can even be applied to your career. We're used to being asked in interviews, 'Where do you see yourself in five years' time?' but how many of us have actually taken time to plan those five (ten, fifteen, ...) years? Anybody serious about their career should really plan several years ahead, look to their ultimate goal, see the next step or two in their career and work out their route. Just think about all the work Baelish must have done before he actually put his plan into action. The most successful careerists create more than one plan and constantly revise and rework their strategies. In an uncertain world this is the only way to maintain a measure of control.

By engaging in scenario planning individuals and organizations can take some of the uncertainty out of the future. Not only that, they can to an extent direct events so that they play towards their strengths. By learning from the past and constantly assessing and reassessing the situation in the Seven Kingdoms even before the War of the Five Kings broke out, the Lannisters were able to master their destiny, at least for a while, whereas the Starks, who trusted in virtue and rectitude were tossed aside by the hand of fate.

15

DON'T OVERSHARE

Ned Stark: *"Lord Baelish, perhaps I was wrong to distrust you."*
Petyr Baelish: *"Distrusting me was the wisest thing you've done since you climbed off your horse."*

As an ambitious careerist or entrepreneur you always have several plans on the go. It can be helpful to share these plans – sometimes it's even necessary – but be very careful who you talk to and what you tell them. For instance if, say, you're planning to call the inheritance of the throne into question because the dead king's son is actually the product of an incestuous liasion between the queen and her brother, and you plan to put the old king's brother on the throne instead, the person to tell probably isn't an ambitious schemer who's had his eye on your wife since they were teenagers. Especially when he's told you not to trust him.

When Cat Stark suspects the Lannisters of plotting to finish off Bran she tells a select group of just four people her suspicions: her eldest son, his best friend and the family's two faithful old retainers. When her husband Ned discovers the truth about Joffrey's parentage, and what seems to be the reason for John Arryn's murder, he realizes he cannot achieve anything on his own. But unlike Cat he has nobody obvious to trust. Having spent so much time away from King's Landing he's out of the loop when it comes to intrigue and doesn't have anybody he can naturally turn to in this situation. Recognizing Baelish as another outsider and knowing he's somebody his wife has trusted in the past he tries to recruit him to his cause, discussing his plans with him. He only truly realizes the enormity of his error later when Baelish's dagger is at his throat and by then, of course, it is too late.

You're unlikely to intentionally share your most important secrets with somebody you don't know very well, but what about contacts in your industry, colleagues or even your employer? It may seem petty, but before you start sharing your company-transforming ideas with your boss or co-workers over a friendly pint, or reveal your latest bright idea at your next networking meet-up, take a moment to consider this – whose success does your eager listener most want, yours? Or theirs?

These days the watchword is 'transparency'. You could be forgiven for thinking that in order for a business to succeed it needs to be completely open about all its dealings. But clearly a line has to be drawn. Some secrets should never be shared: imagine if we all knew the Colonel's original recipe of eleven herbs and spices or the secret behind Coca-Cola's unique flavour. These secrets give KFC and Coca-Cola not only a product that cannot be precisely imitated but also a mystique which sets them apart from copycat rivals.

But if a business is completely secretive, makes too little information about itself available or makes itself difficult to approach it can lead to suspicion among potential consumers. If you're prepared to gain customer loyalty in other ways, the most obvious example being by taking a leaf out of Amazon's book and making yourself considerably cheaper than your rivals, then that's fine. But if you're unwilling or unable to reduce your margins you need to be more open and approachable. While some customers will always choose the cheaper option regardless of other factors, in many industries a sufficient number of customers will be lured by great customer service and an ethical way of doing business: being open with your customers can be a cost-free way of gaining and retaining business if you do it right. As well as sharing with customers all the things you are doing well it's also a good idea to acknowledge the things you are not so good at and the steps you have put in place to improve your performance: if you know that a significan number of people that use your business are experiencing delays in delivery of your goods and services the worst thing you can do is act as if nothing is wrong, since it looks as though you don't care.

In many cases it's not so much a case of whether you share as when you do it. If you launch a new product or service and it is successful competitors will always try to imitate it – Apple may have launched the first successful tablet computer and Netflix was the first subscription-based DVD by mail service but they did not remain the only examples in their respective markets for long. But one thing that has Appleophiles queuing up for days to buy the company's latest product is the secrets they share.

For months, even years, before a new product is launched there are tantalizing rumours, which are never credited to an actual inside source ('psst – we heard that Apple's next product is going to be a watch that works in synch with your iPhone'). At this stage you can bet that all Apple's competitors call together their R&D departments demanding that they drop everything and start devising wearable tech. But by then it is too late – they're already years behind the soon to be market leaders. We then have the big launch where the product is displayed in all its glory and a launch date at just the right point in the future is announced – just long enough to increase the hype to fever pitch but not so long that we all get bored and start obsessing about some other 'must-have' device. So good is Apple at knowing what to share when that its watch was listed as one of *Time*'s 25 best inventions of 2014 in spite of the fact that it wasn't available to buy until 2015.

Sharing just enough to get people interested while not sharing so much that you lose your competitive advantage is an art. When it comes to your own career try following Apple's example and not revealing your ideas until you're ready to put them into practice. If you come to your boss with just the germ of an idea there are several potential outcomes. Perhaps you tell her the idea and she lets you run with it but then you work it through only to discover that it's a poor idea. Strike one against you, and if this happens more than once you start to look like a source of poor ideas. The second option is that it turns out to be a great idea but as you involved your boss from the start she's able to claim some or all of the credit for your idea, depending on how cut-throat she is. Which is going to niggle.

Clearly though you can't answer the question, 'What are you working on at the moment?', with 'Oh this and that' and a mysterious grin. Why not take a leaf out of Baelish's book then. He tells Ned just enough about himself and his plans to gain Ned's trust but not so much that Ned would ever have anything to use against him. If you want to play really dirty in business this is a great way of gaining access to your less savvy colleagues' ideas. You tell them a little bit about what you're planning (real or invented) and they – if you've played your cards right – give away their great ideas. If you develop a talent for this you need never sweat away creating any of your own ideas again.

16

GETTING YOUR MESSAGE ACROSS

Maester Aemon: *"Fetch a quill and inkwell ... We had forty-four ravens at last count; make sure they're all fed. Every one of them flies tonight."*

It's tricky trying to get messages around in the Seven Kingdoms, which seem to lack a basic postal or parcel delivery service, even in the cities – and no one has email. They don't even have social media. But they make a pretty good job of it.

Long distance message-passing is done by attaching a letter to a raven. According to the books, the value of a carrier-raven was taught to the First Men of Westeros by the Children of The Forest. At this point the birds could talk, which would have ensured an even higher quality of service. A verbal message is encrypted (it exists in the raven's little brain, and so is harder to intercept without catching every passing raven and torturing it with tiny instruments). It would also have been easier to direct the message to the person who needs to read it, because you could have told the ravens that your letter was urgent, so no hanging around scavenging, for example. This scavenging thing, it seems, would be an argument in favour of pigeons. Pigeons fly direct, without stopping to feast on corpses (of which there are a lot in *Game of Thrones*).

With this constraint, the rulers of Westeros have become extremely adept at communicating the Big Ideas. They really get the value of symbolism as a way to make a point efficiently. There's a phrase in advertising: 'show, don't tell'. So, if you want to make thousands of people afraid of you, don't make long speeches telling them to be afraid, or write lots of nasty letters and attach them to every raven you can find. You do something unexpected that should make them think: watch out.

Pouring molten gold on an ambitious person's head, walking into your husband's burning funeral pyre and walking out again the next day to show that you're a bit special, or chopping off the hand of the best swordsman just to show everyone that you can, isn't necessarily a communications strategy to follow at home or the office. But, in the real world, communications directors who work for our largely ignored politicians, who weep silently as they arrange another tired visit to a small factory somewhere in the industrial heartlands so that their boss can be filmed in a hi-vis jacket pretending to know what the machine does, must wish they lived in Westeros from time to time.

Niccolo Machiavelli serves as a useful link between *Game of Thrones* and our world. In *The Prince*, he relates how Pope

Alexander VI cleaned up the Romagna province. With a weak government and crime everywhere, the Pope sent Remirro de Orco, his fixer, to clean house by punishing lots of people harshly and cruelly. Everyone hated Remirro, because he was good at what he did: Romagnan crime rates dropped, with a large amount of bloodshed along the way. So, when the job was done, 'Alexander had him cut in half, and placed one morning in the public square'. Result: everyone liked that there was less crime, and they liked the Pope even more. Remirro showed that no one is above the law, but Alexander showed that no one was above the Pope.

Here lies the difference between sending a message and making a gesture. When a political leader is photographed pointing at something while wearing a hard hat, it no longer sends us any strong message, because it is what we expect. It delivers no new information. If we even notice, we shrug. A strong message is easiest to convey when it implies new clarity and unexpected change, even if only for a few people. That's why the most memorable messages often emerge from disorder and confusion, and why most big gestures in our world are so forgettable.

17

PLAYING THE WAITING GAME

Cersei Lannister: *"A good king knows when to save his strength and when to destroy his enemies."*

Of all the hot-tempered, macho men in Westeros the Stark boys are probably the worst. As Petyr Baelish notes, they have quick tempers and slow minds. They're not really stupid but they are so impatient to act they generally don't give themselves enough time to assess a situation and work out the best course of action. Baelish himself on the other hand must have been plotting his strategy for years. Ned's readiness to plunge into a fight made it easy for Baelish to play him, starting the War of the Five Kings. But Stannis Baratheon is also rather hot tempered. If you thought somebody else was stealing your throne you'd probably be keen to rectify the situation but Stannis may have been able to take King's Landing at the Battle of Blackwater Bay if he'd waited until he had more troops at his disposal to overpower the city forces. As it was he decided to plough ahead even when the large Tyrell forces refused to swear allegiance to him. The fact that the Tyrells then decided to join forces with the Lannisters meant that Stannis was ultimately unsuccessful in his attempt to take the city.

Daenerys on the other hand has spent four entire series biding her time in Essos. She's learning how to rule, mustering her manpower and hopefully improving her chances of success when she finally does cross the Narrow Sea. By managing not to get involved in any war for the kingdom as yet she's been able to conserve her resources. With the other contenders for the throne killing one another off and racking up huge bills in the process she may be able to benefit greatly from pacing herself. But she needs to stay focused – she doesn't want to miss her opportunity.

Had Stannis been successful he would have gained the throne and thereby been able to repel other contenders; as it is he could have made the way easier for his opponents. It's the risk you take when you make the first move. You're probably aware of the idea of first-mover advantage; that by being the first to market with a particular product or service you gain an advantage that your competitors can't surmount. By creating the market you become the name synonymous with it and thereby control it. Coca-Cola, for example, is likely the first name that comes to mind when you think of cola drinks. They were the first to begin selling that product and have continued to market it as the authentic cola drink (including advertising it as 'the real thing'), helping it to be the favoured cola for more than 100 years.

The Dyson name is synonymous with cyclonic vacuum cleaners and is a beautifully designed, carefully patented product with an inventor–owner who has managed to make himself the heart of the product. But is it always an advantage to be first to market? What are the first names that spring to mind when you see these three product types: social media, search engine, safety razor? No doubt your list is Six Degrees, Archie, and the Star Safety Razor. No? Why not? These were the first of their kind available but this perhaps demonstrates the advantages of waiting – second- (or even third-) mover advantage. Facebook, Google and Gillette were able to learn from the originators in terms both of what they did well and what they did less well. Think about it for a minute and you'll see that there can be sound reasons for not being first. Imagine you are developing a product. You have a great idea but then before it's ready to be sold you have to create prototypes, test them out, refine the product. As the Dyson web site proudly states the cleaners we see now are, 'the result of 5,127 prototypes and 15 years of frustration and perseverance'. All those prototypes cost a lot of money, meaning James Dyson was $4 million in debt before his product found a market, and it's a common story. Dyson was lucky but many companies run out of money before they have a chance to capitalize on their hard work. This leaves the way clear for others to pick up where they left off, benefiting from the originator's experience and saving themselves time and money.

Next, you have to convince people to buy the product. You have to show them its benefits, make them see that they need it in their lives, market it, advertise. But as second mover the hard work of convincing people has already been done. When James

Dyson first started trying to sell his product he was told there was no market for a bagless cleaner – the very thing he was using as his selling point. The market was firmly entrenched in the idea that vacuum cleaners had to have bags. Not only that but many vacuum cleaner manufacturers relied on the huge market for vacuum cleaner bags so a bagless cleaner threatened their business model. In this particular instance James Dyson managed to gain advantage as the first mover once he finally sold a few cleaners and customers began to see the benefits, but only after many years and at great expense. Others have not fared so well, finding that they have spent all their money on creating a market that is then swiped away from them by a less cash-strapped second mover.

Sadly many first movers are small companies or individual entrepreneurs who have too little funding to complete the journey with their innovation. And a lot of second movers turn out to be well-funded, established companies. So it's pleasing to note that James Dyson successfully sued Hoover for copyright infringement when that company tried to steal his first-mover advantage from him.

There are advantages and disadvantages for both first and second movers. This can apply not only to business ideas but to your individual career. Yes, you're impatient, you have a limited amount of time in which to scale the career heights and could be forgiven for wanting to press ahead, and often this energy and drive can lead to success. However, sometimes hanging back, watching how others fail and learning from their mistakes can benefit you. Just because you were not the first it doesn't mean you can't be the ultimate victor.

18

ACT ON EVIDENCE NOT ON PREJUDICE

Brienne: *"I'm not interested in foul rumours."*
Jaime: *"Unless they're about me."*

Characters in *Game of Thrones* are frequently misjudged because they are young, female or smaller than average while others are judged by what people think they know about them. If you base your behaviour towards a colleague or a rival on their obvious attributes could you be missing something?

So your boss has picked you for the new project – great! Problem is he wants you to work with somebody you can't stand. Well if you're honest you don't really know him but you've heard about him from others – he's arrogant, overprivileged and rumours are that he was instrumental in the ousting of his previous manager – so you aren't looking forward to it. But if you want this job you're going to have to suck it up and get on with it. Besides, you never know, he may not turn out to be as bad as you've been led to believe.

When Catelyn Stark charges Brienne of Tarth with the task of conveying Jaime Lannister safely to King's Landing, as a bargaining tool for the safe return of her daughters, Brienne is not happy, but her sworn allegiance to Catelyn means she takes on the task. By reputation Jaime is arrogant and untrustworthy, he is rumoured to be sleeping with his own sister and killed King Aerys by, quite literally, stabbing him in the back, earning him the epithet 'Kingslayer'. However, in the course of their journey the two are forced to get to know one another and by the time they finally reach King's Landing have formed a friendship (in fact at least on Brienne's side it is more than that) and despite ourselves we have come to like Jaime more too.

Like Brienne we dislike Jaime from the start because we don't know him. But as he himself wonders, "Why do you hate me so much? Have I ever harmed you?" He is arrogant and self-assured, knowing that the Lannister name will open doors for him. What little we do know about him tells us he is untrustworthy and indeed cruel, pushing Bran from the tower with a breezy, "The things I do for love". Perhaps he hadn't had a chance to prove himself, perhaps it's time away from his sister's malign influence or perhaps a year spent in prison made him a little less self-satisfied. He certainly reveals a different, kinder, more noble side to his nature on the journey back to King's Landing. He saves Brienne from being gang raped by Locke's men before his overconfidence in his powers of persuasion loses him his sword hand. This event changes him and he decides to give up and die until Brienne tells him to pull himself together. But he surprises even himself when he returns to Harrenhal to rescue Brienne from Locke (and a bear) once again.

For his part Jaime, like everybody else, judges Brienne on her appearance – a very tall woman dressed in armour and pretending to be a knight? Why – that's hilarious. But he comes to see that she is actually a very skilled swordswoman, fighting and killing three Stark soldiers before besting him in a swordfight.

Jaime was head of the Kingsguard but killed the king. In so doing he dealt the final stroke for the rebellion yet Robert and Ned both rather snootily despise him as less noble than they are, perhaps recognizing that he could just as easily turn on them if it became inconvenient to support them. Ned says, "You served Aerys well when serving was safe," implying that he's opportunistic rather than honourable. But Jaime reveals to Brienne what he's never told anybody else, that Aerys had (a) commanded him to bring him Tywin's head, (b) planted stores of wildfire around the castle and capital intending to burn everyone. In fact his dying words were "Burn them all!" – mad indeed. So in fact Jaime had to kill him otherwise he'd have had the death of most of the city's population on his conscience.

Through getting to know each other properly Jaime discovers a relationship that isn't about either sex or one-upmanship and Brienne gains a sword of valyrian steel, a new suit of armour and a bumbling squire (and a new crush).

So make sure you know your allies and your competition – from rival companies to members of your team. Don't assume that because somebody is young or new to the business they can be disregarded, and don't presume to judge somebody on hearsay. Gossiping at the watercooler is not networking! If somebody tells you the new director is a slavedriver she may well be, but equally the person giving you this information may have been used to an easy ride under the previous manager and isn't thrilled at having finally to do some work. If you're already the most hard working member of your team this could be your chance to impress. Should you hear on the grapevine that the other person applying for the promotion you're after is an air-head who can't do his current job don't let that affect your approach to the promotion in question – the rumours may be true but if you believe them and go into the interview acting like the job's already yours you'll look arrogant and unprofessional – traits unlikely to impress. And if, whether as a colleague or as a manager, you participate in mockery of 'different' team members then that's bullying, and a very serious matter indeed.

The more audacious out there will realize that if others listen to gossip but you don't you might be able to employ this to your advantage and start rumours yourself. Tyrion does this to root out spies by sharing 'information' in confidence with those he suspects and then seeing which rumour travels. Littlefinger runs a concerted campaign against Ned, feeding him both information and misinformation. This tactic is really only for very advanced game-players, but if you're feeling particularly sneaky and know what you're doing then playing on assumption and prejudice can be incredibly helpful.

Be smart, be circumspect and for gods' sake be nice: when everybody else is gossiping and bitching it'll take you a lot further than you might expect.

19

KEEP IT IN THE FAMILY

Tywin Lannister: *"The house that puts family first will always defeat the house that puts the whims and wishes of its sons and daughters first. A good man does everything in his power to better his family's position."*

We can safely say that Tywin Lannister is a man without sentimentality. Nevertheless he does send Jaime and 30,000 of his troops to rescue his other son, Tyrion, from the Eyrie, much to Jaime's astonishment. When Jaime questions why Tywin would devote so many resources to the son he seems to despise Tywin sets him straight – his decision has nothing to do with Tyrion and everything to do with family honour. Not rescuing him would have made the Lannisters look weak. For the same reason Yara Greyjoy attempts to rescue her utterly worthless brother from Ramsay Snow (though her father points out his literal familial pointlessness now he's been separated from his 'favourite toy'). There are times when you have to put aside your personal feelings for the benefit of the organization or your larger plan.

The divisions in *Game of Thrones* are drawn along family lines, but not everybody seems to prioritize family over all else in quite the same way as Tywin Lannister does. For example Ned Stark tells his younger daughter, Arya, that they are living in dangerous times: "winter is truly coming and in the winter we must protect ourselves; look after one another." But then his actions seem to suggest he accords the realm greater importance than his family. If he really thought family was the most important thing wouldn't the best thing he could do be to stay alive? Instead he sets out on a path to prove the illegitimacy of Cersei's children; a mission that gets him branded a traitor and executed. The Stark family becomes, to those loyal to the crown, that of a traitor. One daughter has to flee for her life, while the other remains at court to be tormented by Joffrey. Ned's eldest son, Robb, leads the Northerners to war, leaving Bran, who's 10, in charge of Winterfell, which gets sacked and burned by Ramsay Snow. Without Ned there to tell him not to Robb makes the foolish error of following the whims and wishes of his heart and marrying Talisa rather than pursuing the less palatable but more politically astute path of marrying one of Walder Frey's daughters.

Meanwhile, individual members of the Lannister clan may be miserable, and furious with Daddy, but they are all alive and the family is firmly in charge of the realm. That is until Joffrey is murdered (by another politically astute family, the Tyrells) and Cersei, putting personal feelings ahead of family, siezes the opportunity to have Tyrion accused of the crime. Knowing the importance

Tywin places on the Lannister name and his dream of creating a dynasty that will last a thousand years, Jaime strikes a bargain with Tywin that he will leave the Kingsguard, a role which forbids him from having a family, if Tywin grants Tyrion mercy and sends him to the Wall as his punishment rather than having him executed. If Tyrion is killed, Jaime will remain a Kingsguard and the Lannister name will die. Unfortunately Tyrion is so incensed by Shae's betrayal that despite Jaime's word that he will not be killed his rage leads him to call for trial by combat instead. The whole sorry mess ends with Tywin being killed by his son. Despite all he'd caused Tyrion to suffer he really didn't think he'd kill him because "you're my son" and he thinks he has drummed into his children the importance of family above all else. Tywin's last words? "You shot me! You're no son of mine!" It looks likely now that the kingdom will slip even further into the chaos that Petyr Baelish so relishes.

Threats to family, then, don't always come from outside and it's the same with business. Former Manchester United manager, Alex Ferguson, the English football Premier League's most successful manager of all time can put a lot of his success down to his unwavering focus on team success no matter what. He had many famous and talented football players in his team over the years and dealing with a locker room full of such egos can't have been easy. No player was more starry than David Beckham.

Beckham came through the ranks from the United youth team, which he joined in 1991, to become one of the most famous footballers in the world. But it would seem that by 2003 he'd started to act like he was more important than the team. Ferguson realized that if he allowed Beckham to continue believing this it would be very bad for team morale and could jeopardize United's success that season. They'd already lost the League Cup to Liverpool and were trailing in the league to Arsenal who had also put them out of the FA Cup. In the Champions League they faced Real Madrid in a must-win match if they were to keep alive their hopes of any trophy that season. So the last thing you'd expect would be for Fergie to drop the star player from the starting line-up. But that's precisely what he did – Beckham spent most of the game sitting on the bench. When he was finally brought on he scored twice: first from a free kick, with the second goal in injury time. He might have thought he was making a point about his value to the club but actually Fergie had done two things. First of all he'd 'played' Beckham, knowing anger would spur him on to prove something, and more importantly he'd shown that nobody is bigger than the team. Beckham was sold at the end of the season but Manchester United's success continued without him, with the team winning five league titles under Ferguson after Beckham's departure.

Making decisions based on the long view and on the good of your organization or team is not easy and it might not make you popular with those who feel they are victims of your pragmatic approach. And as Tywin's fate demonstrates you need to know where to draw the line between pragmatism and tyranny. A leader who can successfully make this distinction, as Sir Alex ably demonstrated, will achive great things.

20

YOU DON'T KNOW EVERYTHING

Benjen Stark: *"You've never been north of the Wall. So don't tell me what's out there."*

Winter is coming, and with it the White Walkers. It's so long since one of these has been seen that nobody alive can remember them, in fact most people now believe them to be myths. Even when the evidence for their existence starts piling up and the Free Folk begin to head south in flight those in power fail to take their existence seriously, especially as they're already busily involved in manifestly real threats such as civil war and the coming winter. Clearly the time is approaching when they will regret their assumptions. You can't know everything, so make sure you listen to your experts and pay attention to their advice.

Very few characters in the *Game of Thrones* universe take the threat from beyond the Wall seriously. Having never seen a

White Walker themselves most people have grown up thinking of them as stories, in the same category as "grumpkins and snarks and all the other monsters your wet nurse warned you about". Even when others tell them they have seen the Walkers or evidence of them they assume the other person is crazy – Ned Stark refers to the Ranger he has to execute in the first episode as a 'madman'. It's usually only when people see a Walker, or the zombie-like wights they turn their human victims into, that they start to believe in them, and by then it's usually too late.

The Free Folk living north of the Wall have seen enough evidence of the Walkers' existence for them to unite under Mance Rayder and follow him south. But no noble in King's Landing is going to believe the evidence of people they think of as savage Wildlings. Only those in the North are concerned about the southward movement of this huge group and they see it as a threat rather than a warning. Fortunately one potential king is listening to his adviser, and that adviser is getting her information from a higher power.

When Stannis Baratheon receives the message sent out by the Night's Watch to the nobles of Westeros imploring that they send help against the horrors advancing from beyond the Wall he, like all the other nobles is sceptical of the reality of such a threat. Melissandre, the Red Woman, throws the message into the fire to find out what The Lord of Light makes of it and it is only after her verdict, "This War of Five Kings means nothing. The true war lies to the north, my King. Death marches on the Wall. Only you can stop it," that he starts to take the news seriously. While it might be foolish to trust in the supernatural, not to mention some of the sacrifices required by this Lord of Light (and we're still not sure of Melissandre's motives), in this instance Stannis is right to listen to her. And to make sure he listens Melissandre throws in a bit of flattery – only *you* can stop it.

It's not always easy to convince people, especially if you don't have some divinity fighting your corner. While we're on the subject of walls, in October 1929 the Wall Street Crash that brought about twelve years of Great Depression took place. For nearly three years prior to the market collapse economist Roger Babson had been warning that the bull market was inflated and likely to bring about a dangerous crash. In August 1929 he stated that the stock market was heading for a 60 to 80 point crash. This spooked some investors and led to a 3% decline in the stock market at the start of September. The market appeared to rally from this, fell slightly again and rallied again before the eventual crash at the end of October. Wise investors had realized the downward trend and begun to sell; when the rest of the investors realized what was going on they followed suit, creating panic that caused the crash. Among the main causes of the crash were a failure to see the stock market in the wider economic context and observe that its bullishness was out of line with the state of the economy as a whole. But a more important factor was ignorance.

The 1920s were a boom time for industry. The US and its allies had won the First World War in 1918; people were confident and optimistic. The stock market seemed a great way to get rich quickly, and uneducated investors began buying and trading stocks without really understanding the system or knowing much about the companies they were investing in – they simply followed market trends. This would have been bad enough on its own but some groups of people who did know the market saw this as an opportunity to trade stocks between them, making certain stocks look like good prospects to the ignorant mass of investors who then bought them and traded them on to other unwise investors, with their value going up with every trade. The herd that bought the stocks without knowing really what they were doing was the same herd that panicked as the market began to decline and made the mass exit that caused the crash. Babson was not the only economist who warned that the market needed to 'calm the hell down', but he was definitely in a minority, a party pooper saying things nobody wanted to hear. It was the worst economic crisis America has ever seen. Who knows what horrors the inhabitants of Westeros will see visited upon them as a result of their failure to realize their own ignorance.

You cannot know everything about every business situation you find yourself in so don't pretend you do. When you find yourself out of your comfort zone don't just blunder blindly ahead. Find trustworthy people who can explain things to you, listen to what they say, and then, when you do understand the situation you can take action with a far better chance of success.

21

RIGHT IS NOT GOOD ENOUGH

Cersei Lannister: *"Some day you will sit on the throne and the truth will be what you make it."*

As Hand of the King, Ned Stark investigates the circumstances behind the murder of Jon Arryn (the previous Hand). During his investigations he learns what Jon discovered and died for – that Cersei's children were fathered by Jaime not Robert and are therefore not heirs to the throne. He tells her what he knows and threatens to reveal her secret to all unless she leaves King's Landing. When Robert is fatally wounded under suspicious circumstances while hunting he names Joffrey as his heir and Ned as Lord Protector, but Ned alters the edict to say 'the rightful heir' rather than naming Joffrey. Thinking he has the City Watch on his side he challenges Joffrey's kingship and hands Barristan Selmy Robert's last will, which Cersei promptly destroys. Foolish Ned: he should have known that's not the way kingdoms are won; power trumps right every time. The same could be said for business – you can't beat the powerful just by being right.

The Starks are in the right. As men of honour they always take the moral high ground and are disappointed when others turn out to lack their high principles. Clearly they, rather than a madman, a drunk or a sadistic boy, should be ruling the country. If they were in charge everybody would be treated fairly and justly and the poor would be looked after. (But at what price? You just know they'd be knocking on your door every night to make sure you'd said your prayers and you didn't have a local dairymaid hidden under your bed. Although virtuous, this 'Winter is coming' lot are not much fun.)

It's strange that Ned Stark, a man who's experienced war, rebellion, infidelity (on his part) and the brutality of a king who would let his son steal a man's sister and then burn alive her father and brother when they came to rescue her, is so utterly trusting in the power of right, of high morals triumphing. How did he manage to remain so naive? Well, it's probably not so much naivety as his self-righteous anger preventing him from thinking straight.

Ned believes that his piece of paper is sufficient to stop Joffrey becoming king. This, in a world where one claimant to the throne will use witchcraft to kill his brother and a man will get his would-be lover to kill her husband in order to start off a war seems patently ridiculous. Is it objectively 'wrong' for Joffrey to become king? Or, to put it another way, was it 'right' for Robert to rise up against the previous king and overthrow him? Was it right for Aegon the Conqueror to take control of Westeros 300 years ago? No, as Jorah explains he did it simply 'because he could'. To expect to enforce rules with a piece of paper in a world where they are routinely broken with a sword is plain daft.

Now we're not counselling you to forget your morals to get ahead in business or suggesting that in a world without honour it's OK to do that. The world would be a much worse place if we all behaved like Stannis Baratheon and Petyr Baelish. Sometimes you have to do the right thing and hang the consequences for you simply because more people will suffer if you don't. People who knew about the wrongdoings of the banks prior to the most recent financial crisis and said nothing were probably in the wrong, but sometimes doing 'the right thing' seems to have little effect.

Edward Snowden is a former private intelligence contractor for the NSA who revealed in June 2013 that the US had undertaken some unconstitutional or immoral surveillance of its citizens. He revealed methods used to obtain this intelligence via newspaper articles written by Laura Poitras and Glenn Greenwald. He had become shocked at the amount of surveillance the government was undertaking into ordinary citizens' lives. Having been unable to make his concerns heard in the NSA he went to the press, initially wanting to remain anonymous but then asking the journalists to reveal his identity in order to spare his ex-colleagues from a witch-hunt. Many now see him as a hero for truth, while his country sees him as a traitor. What would you have done in his position?

It would appear that little has so far changed as a result of his revelations – of two court actions taken as a result of his revelations one has ruled the NSA's surveillance 'probably unconstitutional' and the other ruled it 'legal'. Arguably the people most impressed by his actions were those who already assumed the US government (and other governments) were undertaking these kinds of activities. On the other hand, some people may feel that a few slight invasions of privacy are a small price to pay if it helps to put some terrorists out of action. The rest of the population probably just went back to updating Facebook and Twitter with the minute details of their lives. There's no indication that the governments have stopped this surveillance and there's some suggestion that a few terrorist groups have been able to work out new ways to evade surveillance as a result. Snowden himself is living in Russia to avoid arrest, presumably constantly looking over his shoulder for the CIA. So what he did may have had noble motives but was it worth it? Even with the backing of several liberal-minded newspapers Snowden was not really in a position of power so no matter how right his motives may have been his actions seem so far to have had results far less spectacular than the consequences for himself.

There is of course a crucial difference between Ned Stark and Edward Snowden, in terms of their motivation. It seems that Ned was merely motivated by a pernickety need to stick to the rules and uphold the law of succession. Edward Snowden on the other hand seems to have acted out of concern for the lives of his fellow citizens. Of course he must have realised that by acting as he did his own circumstances would become a lot worse. Which makes Snowden's actions heroic while Ned's appear foolhardy. A world where everybody acted only out of self-interest would be a miserable place indeed. But moral decisions are rarely clean-cut. If you find yourself in a situation where you need to choose between toeing the line or blowing the whistle you need not just to know that you are right but also to understand what the consequences, good and bad, might be. Your actions will depend on the relative strengths of the moralist and pragmatist in you. And to be sure of achieving anything you have to be in a very strong position.

22

EVERYBODY HAS A WEAKNESS

Rakharo: *"My father taught me how to fight. He taught me that speed defeats size."*

As the series progresses it starts to look like the Lannisters have it all sewn up, but even they have weaknesses; infighting, incest and a rapidly emptying purse being among them. Sooner or later somebody will be able to exploit these. On a grander scale it would seem that the Seven Kingdoms are impenetrable from the north, what with that 300 mile long, 700 foot high solid ice wall in the way, but we've already seen how a determined group of Free Folk could circumvent it. Even the White Walkers have a weakness – should you have a spearhead made of dragonglass about your person they're easily defeated.

Faced with separating Kraznys, the ruler of Astapor, from his slave army of Unsullied, Daenerys has two challenges. First she disapproves of slavery, second she only has a small band of Dothraki and could not take the highly trained slave army by force. She both acquires the Unsullied army and frees them by using the ruler's arrogance and disrespect for her against him. Believing she cannot speak his language Kraznys persistently insults her, making her determined to better him. She exchanges the slaves for Drogon, the largest of her dragons, but when he hands her the whip to control the Unsullied she commands them to kill the masters and free the slaves. Drogon on the other hand will not respond to Kraznys' commands. Unfortunately for him Drogon is not a slave. The only person he responds to is his mother, Daenerys. So she tells him to burn Kraznys alive. Kraznys made the classic error of underestimating somebody because they seemed like an unworthy foe. His fatal mistake was to assume Daenerys didn't speak his language and couldn't negotiate because she is merely a girl. Daenerys had similar successes in Yunkai, which she took by sending three men in through the poorly guarded back gate, and Meereen, where she employed subterfuge to get the slaves inside the city to take it from within. By using unconventional methods you can turn your disadvantages into advantages.

As Malcolm Gladwell points out in his book *David and Goliath: Underdogs, Misfits and the Art of Battling Giants*, 'Giants are not what we think they are. The same qualities that give them strength are often the sources of great weakness ... Power can come in other forms ... in breaking rules, in substituting speed and surprise for strength.' He goes on to back this up with the example of a survey undertaken by a political scientist called Ivan Arreguín-Toft into the odds of small armies beating a larger foe in war. Examining wars fought in the last 200 years between foes with a discrepancy in size of at least tenfold he noted that while the larger side was the victor 71.5% of the time, when the smaller side refused to meet the larger one on its terms, for example by employing guerrilla tactics, the smaller side was victorious 63.6% of the time.

If you think about this in terms of business for a while you begin to see that while larger, established companies do have advantages in terms of size of workforce, reach, experience and funds available they also have weaknesses such as entrenched attitudes, sluggish systems and complicated processes. So one way a small company can compete is through 'disruptive innovation'. This is a theory proposed in the 1990s by Clayton Christensen to describe the situation when a new product or service changes the market, replacing what was there before with something new. He noted that while larger businesses might well be aware of the disruptive innovation they find it hard to respond to it. They might not believe it's worth their attention or see the need to respond quickly or at all; after all what they have been doing has worked for years. Alternatively while they may see the need to respond they try to fit the new thinking into an old way of working, an old framework within which the innovation cannot work.

The video rental chain Blockbuster fell victim to this type of thinking rather spectacularly. Since its establishment in the 1980s Blockbuster had worked on the same model: customers visited their stores and borrowed a film for a fixed period of time before returning it. Late returns incurred 'late fees'. In 1999, fed up with being charged late fees Reed Hastings set up a new company based on a different model. Instead of hiring individual films Netflix's customers signed up to a subscription model. For a fixed monthy fee they could borrow as many films as they wanted; the DVDs arrived in the mail and were returned in a pre-paid envelope and there were no late fees.

Blockbuster was certainly aware of Netflix, it just didn't recognize that the model was a game-changer. At one point in 2000 Reed Hastings even tried to sell the company to Blockbuster for $50 million but the owner of Blockbuster at the time, John Antioco, practically laughed the Netflix team out of the office. Even so, there were several other opportunities for Blockbuster to purchase Netflix, all of which were dismissed. Instead Blockbuster tried other ventures including an ill-starred deal with Enron Broadband Services, which it had to drop after scandal hit Enron. It did eventually jump on the DVD by mail bandwagon but very late in the day. When Blockbuster filed for bankruptcy in 2010 it was valued at $24 million, while Netflix, which had changed the market irreversibly in the space of 11 years, was estimated to be worth $13 billion.

The problem for Blockbuster was not a new technology but a new model. Initially the company did not see Netflix's model as a serious contender – they thought people would still want to rent movies from their stores. Once they did understand the disruption they didn't have the wherewithal to deal with it – having been focused on one model for so long they found it too difficult to switch to the new way of doing things. In 2011 Netflix was faced with a similar challenge itself due to the growing popularity of streaming films. Reed Hastings worried his business would meet the same fate as Blockbuster. In a blog he said, 'Most companies that are great at something do not become great at new things people want (streaming for us) because they are afraid to hurt their initial business.' Clearly this self-awareness helped; after a period of indecision over how to react Netflix seems to have managed to make the two models coexist, with the streaming model now having overtaken its original DVD rental service in terms of revenue as the market once again makes an irreversible shift.

23

DELEGATE

Jaime Lannister: *"What's the line? 'The King shits and The Hand wipes.'"*

Tywin Lannister is a born leader. He has many flaws but he is a superb delegator, and his younger son Tyrion has learned much (both dos and do nots) by observing him. Tywin's heir is Jaime, but Jaime is not a leader – becoming Hand of the King is an honour he "can do without". Individualistic and a bit wayward, all he really wants to do is fight and he would far rather be in charge of the Kingsguard than the kingdom. When you're delegating it's best to leave personal feelings out of the decision; it sounds obvious but you have to choose the person who's right for the job.

To be fair Hand of the King seems like a rather onerous task. Arguably it makes you the most powerful man in the kingdom; but that also makes you the most hated and vulnerable man.

Even before she knows that Jon Arryn was murdered – by the Lannisters as she is led to believe – Cat Stark begs her husband not to take the job. And Jaime points out to Cersei two good reasons for not finding the position appealing: "Their days are too long, their lives are too short."

Delegation is one of the hardest things for managers to get right. Many leaders find it difficult to delegate because they know that ultimately they are still responsible for a particular project so if it's done badly it will reflect badly on them. Conversely some poor managers find it all too easy to delegate because they misunderstand it as shirking off responsibility – if you give work to somebody and they do it badly it's their fault and they can expect to be yelled at, disciplined or even fired. The first kind of manager finds herself overworked, stressed and deprived from senior roles as she's irreplaceable in the job she has; the second is bitched about endlessly by underlings (her word for them) and passed over for promotion as unprofessional. Clearly it's a skill you need to master if you want to ascend the career ladder.

It would seem that King Robert, while jovial and Henry VIII-like, is also a sloppy leader. Fortunately although he shirks responsibility he also chooses well when he picks his second in command. Robert fought a rebellion to oust the Targaryens who stole his fiancée. Leading an army against the king's forces would have required bravery, a commanding manner and an ability to make tough decisions, but now he's expected to rule he's discovered that leadership is a series of boring decisions. On the route back to King's Landing from the North he voices his frustrations to Ned. Suggesting he could leave the whole court retinue behind and start again, he simultaneously yearns for the good old days and wishes he'd led a different life. So disillusioned with leading is he that he fails to bother turning up at small council meetings, trusting "small matters" – the boring but important stuff – to the council. Maester Pycell points out that King Robert "has many cares" but actually he has many whores, a lot of wine and a hunt to go on. Clearly he recruited Ned as his Hand because he knew he'd be able to abdicate responsibility since he could count on Ned to be diligent and thorough (a little too thorough as it turns out).

Anybody who's worked somewhere where attendance at regular team meetings is expected can sympathize with Robert's boredom – they're prone to be dull and can keep you from what you really want to do – but having won the war Robert should have grown up and taken his leadership seriously. Being out of the loop so much – Ned finds it hard to get messages to him because he's so frequently otherwise engaged – makes it easy for the less benign members of his court to plot against him.

So Robert demonstrates that the type of man who leads armies may not be the right man to make strategic governmental decisions. This requires a different type of leader, not the manly warrior so much as somebody clever and thoughtful. Tyrion has the role of Hand of the King delegated to him by his father as Tywin (who arguably is capable both of leading armies and making more long-term strategic decisions) is too busy leading the Lannister forces to return to King's Landing as Joffrey's Hand after Robert's death. Tyrion, we know, cannot lead an army as he gets knocked down by his own men right at the start of the battle against Robb's forces and misses the whole thing – but he makes a good leader when thought is valued over action.

Although up until the point where he becomes Hand it has appeared that Tyrion is an idle lord's son with interests only in drinking and whoring, we've also seen that he's been preparing for potential leadership. As well as drink and loose women he likes books. Jon Snow (who's probably never read a book in his life and would most likely consider it a pastime for sissies) asks why he reads so much and Tyrion tells him it's because he's a Lannister and things are expected of him: "My brother has a sword and I have a mind and a mind needs books like a sword needs a whetstone."

It's clear then why Tywin chose the son he supposedly despises over the beloved golden boy Jaime. He knew he could count on him to carry out the job well. When required to plan a defence of King's Landing against Stannis Baratheon's fleet he leaves the manly stuff to others and instead uses his cunning to concoct a very successful plan, filling the bay with the wildfire that, once ignited by Bron, sees much of the fleet blown up before the soldiers can come ashore. Despite this, as the battle rages on, it starts to look like Stannis might be about to win after all but this is the point where Tywin takes over. Tyrion had been finding it harder to implement his decisions in the face of resistance from the king and queen regent (but then Cersei hates him and disagrees with him on most things on principle) so this was an opportune moment to take back control. And it makes Tywin look like a hero. As a manager you too may have to do this, though riding in on a white horse and unceremoniously stripping your faithful delagatee of office is probably not the best way of going about it. Naturally you will be more subtle; perhaps thanking them for what they've done, praising their work and rewarding them, if appropriate, would be a better approach.

24

YOU WIN OR YOU DIE

Petyr Baelish: *"So many men, they risk so little. They spend their lives avoiding danger ... and then they die. I'd risk everything to get what I want."*

Baelish is ambitious enough to have thought about how he would behave were he to gain the Iron Throne. In fact he's ambitious enough to have orchestrated the whole War of the Five Kings. As he explains to Sansa when she asks why he killed Joffrey, his immediate goal is to keep his foes confused. As long as they don't know him or his plans he'll be one step ahead of them. "A man with great ambition and no morals", according to Varys, he's not to be underestimated. As Varys tells him, "I wouldn't bet against you." So far he's doing pretty well, and *Game of Thrones* is so adept at confounding our expectations that we wouldn't bet against him either; perhaps the series will turn out to be the story of how a "grasper from a minor house with a major talent for befriending powerful men" became the most powerful man.

As with the game of thrones, when you have business ambitions you have to play to win. Fortunately in business the punishment for failure is rarely death. If you're aiming for the very top, so we're told, there's no room for those who don't commit themselves one hundred per cent. In order to be able to succeed you're going to have to be prepared to fail too – you'll never scale the heights if you play it safe.

Articles on entrepreneurism like to sell us the stories of men and women who risked it all on one final throw of the dice and succeeded. You know, the folks who spent their rent money on one final gamble on the idea they really believed in; the bailiffs were knocking at the door but because of their determination lady luck smiled down on them and they're now billionaires. It makes a good story: James Dyson, inventor of the cyclonic vacuum cleaner, was the equivalent of $4 million in debt, with three mortgages on his house, before anybody bought his product. He has said, 'I liked living on the edge. All those years that my house was in hock to the bank ... I liked the danger, the idea that everything depended on getting that next product right in every way.' (How his wife and children felt might be another matter.) But for every James Dyson there are thousands of would-be entrepreneurs who threw in their last cent chasing a bad idea. Anybody who's ever watched *Dragons' Den*, or its American cousin *Shark Tank*, where would-be entrepreneurs try to persuade successful investors to put thousands of pounds into their businesses, will know that there are far more bad than good inventions out there (SuperKneeS – roller skates for your knees – anybody?) but that doesn't stop their creators believing in them. Self-belief is only one small element of success. Risk takers in *Game of Thrones* end up with their heads on spikes, and taking crazy risks in business is less likely to lead to billions than it is to bankruptcy. If you examine the stories of most successful entrepreneurs you will find that, like Petyr Baelish, they are calculated risk takers.

At Babson College, the top school in the US for entrepreneurship, successful entrepreneur Leonard C. Green teaches his students the best way to take risk. Rather than risking everything on one last roll of the dice, pitting huge rewards against the kind of abject failure from which there is no return, he suggests that they take incremental risks. Not only that but they should try to minimize the time and money they invest in the project so that if they fail the cost to them is far lower. In contrast to leaps of faith, every time you take a small step you can learn from it, making the next step you take even less risky.

Petyr Baelish claims that he is willing to risk everything to get what he wants. (When asked what that is he rather unhelpfully says, "everything" – nothing like having specific, measurable, achievable goals eh, Pete?) But he's actually far more clever than that. First of all he follows the power; he makes sure he's friends with the right people at the right time. At first it was the Lannisters but Joffrey was clearly too unstable and didn't make a good ally. Now he's made sure to be friends with the Tyrells as he sees their star is in the ascendant, so he bestows upon them the 'thoughtful gift' of facilitating Joffrey's murder. Second, because Baelish usually gets other people to do his dirty work he can rarely be linked back to any event. For example he persuaded Lysa Arryn to kill her husband John Arryn and managed to make the Starks think the Lannisters did it anyway. Just to be safe he killed Lysa, so who could trace it back to him?

The poison that killed Joffrey was, unbeknown to Sansa, hidden in a necklace given to her by Dontos Hollard, which she wore at the wedding feast. Baelish himself was out of town at the time so again even if Cersei hadn't decided to blame it all on Tyrion it would have been hard to trace it back to Baelish.

In a less murderous way Bill Gates, often held up as an example of somebody who, by quitting Harvard to start up Microsoft, took a huge risk, can be seen to be a calculated risk taker. To begin with he was from a rich family so even had he simply quit Harvard and then failed it's unlikely he'd have found himself on the breadline. Second, Gates' parents gave him another head start in life by sending him to a prestigious prep school before he was accepted to Harvard, and there he was able to learn about programming (which he wouldn't have been able to do had he been sent to public school). Third, he didn't quit; not to begin with. He gained permission to take a year's leave of absence from his studies to write his BASIC programme and he only did this once the makers of the Altair 8800 (the 'World's First Microcomputer Kit to Rival Commercial Models,') had agreed to purchase the software from him and partner Paul Allen. It took him a further year before he decided that the risks were low enough for him to leave Harvard in favour of devoting himself to Microsoft.

So if you're a budding entrepreneur you don't need to risk your future on one make or break moment. Many of the most successful entrepreneurs started small, worked hard and grew their businesses incrementally. While this may not be such a sexy story, when you replace the unreliable element of luck with commitment, intelligence and graft, success becomes far more achievable for all of us.

25

THE CLIMB

Petyr Baelish: *"Chaos isn't a pit. Chaos is a ladder. Many who try to climb it fail and never get to try again. The fall breaks them. And some are given a chance to climb. They refuse, they cling to the realm, or the gods, or love. Illusions. Only the ladder is real. The climb is all there is."*

Can we control the future? Maybe a better question is, should we even try? Varys and Baelish, or Littlefinger if you will, converse about their ambitions and goals. Varys has no interest in gaining the throne for himself, only in making sure he's always in the right place at the right time. Baelish on the other hand has definitely thought about it. In this speech he dismisses the historical texts as "a story we agree to tell each other over and over, until we forget that it's a lie." It's when Lord Varys points out that the alternative is chaos that Littlefinger gives his speech. He points out that chaos isn't something to fear, not only that but his entire game plan is based around the idea that in the midst of chaos lies opportunity. In fact it's the only way that people outside the system can get any foothold in the Seven Kingdoms.

If the inhabitants of the Seven Kingdoms are fully occupied trying to avoid falling into the pit they believe chaos to be, the environment in which they live doesn't help. When dead people can be reanimated, for example, which must be disorientating. 'Winter is coming', we are told at the beginning, which reminds inhabitants of the time when a previous winter lasted a generation. Why did it do that? Maybe it doesn't matter much if there are undead people coming to kill you as a result.

So Littlefinger has a point: when things change, old certainties become less valuable, less useful, no matter how comforting they are. Yet the idea that our societies and lives are in equilibrium is alluring for all of us.

We build it into the way we teach business, in which the forces of supply and demand balance to create stable prices and employment and growth. Yet, at the same time, we also know this isn't really true. The economist Joseph Schumpeter was the first to identify a process he called 'creative destruction', in which innovation destroys the old world to create a better one. Real entrepreneurs don't just tweak existing ideas, they rip them up and start again. If you do this successfully, you get your reward because you are in a field of one: but the risk of disaster is much greater. Schumpeter realized that disequilibrium is normal. We also now know that this applies in society, or to the weather.

It doesn't even take an entrepreneur to create disequilibrium. In the UK, one in seven workers was made redundant in the five years from the start of the financial crisis in 2008, which would have seemed inconceivable a decade earlier. The chaotic nature of what economists call 'the business cycle' means that we might have a good idea of how secure our jobs will be next month, but no clear answer to the question if we ask about next year, and certainly no idea of the next ten years.

We instinctively value continuity in our lives and our societies, and many of us react irrationally to disruptive change. In a recent experiment, the Royal Statistical Society took people who overestimated the problems of immigration, and confronted them with well-researched facts that contradicted their ideas. The people overwhelmingly decided that the statistics must be wrong.

We all think we wouldn't do the same thing in our lives, but most of us react to sudden change by holding on to the stories we tell ourselves, even if they are not true. Not all of us can be a Littlefinger, climbing the ladder out of chaos, or a Schumpeterian entrepreneur, who creates the ladder in the first place.

We spend our lives in the understandable hope that chaos doesn't come to our homes, families or workplaces. Insurance, savings and sandbags in the shed may help; but to flourish, rather than simply survive, we need to have a little bit of Littlefinger in us, and recognize that clinging exclusively to "the realm, or the gods, or love" will eventually put us on the receiving end of some process of creative destruction.

26

A HOUSE DIVIDED CANNOT STAND

Ned Stark: *"We've come to a dangerous place. We can't fight a war among ourselves."*

When it's revealed that Joffrey is not the rightful heir to the Iron Throne it's clear to Ned Stark that the throne should pass to the elder of Robert Baratheon's two brothers, Stannis. But when he points this out to the younger brother, Renly, he states that he doesn't believe Stannis would be a good king and that he should be king himself. Thus divided, the Baratheons hand an immediate advantage to other contenders when, had they stood together, the Starks would have stood with them and they may well have quashed any chance the Lannisters had of putting their puppet king on the throne.

The inability to deal with dissent effectively is a problem for many of the groups in this War of the Five Kings. When Stannis and Renly take up arms against one another they also go to war against Joffrey, who, although illegitimate, in the eyes of most people is their nephew. When Stannis visits the Iron Bank of Braavos to arrange his loan the bank manager explains how others might view their actions: "The King's grandfather tells ... a story about a jealous uncle, whose attempts to usurp the throne from the rightful king cost the Seven Kingdoms dearly – in blood and gold."

Tywin Lannister's mishandling of Cersei's vengeful strike against Tyrion eventually leads to Tywin's death, and Robb's failure to see the importance of Roose Bolton's dissent proves fatal too. It was the Northern Lords who asked Robb to be their King in the North so one can understand a bit of arrogance on his part. But the Lords are all experienced warriors, while Robb himself has never been in battle before, let alone commanded an army. Roose Bolton sees himself as a pragmatist but his views were seen as heartless and ignoble by Robb. For example Roose had suggested that instead of wasting precious food on Lannister prisoners they should have killed them (well actually, being Roose, he went a stage further and suggested torture). While we can understand Robb's refusal to subject these men to such unnecessary suffering, the more practical part of the advice, that when resources are scarce they should go to the Northern soldiers not prisoners of war, makes sense, at least on a purely statistical level. More importantly Robb seemed unaware that by dismissing Roose's advice and taking the pretty but difficult high road he was making an enemy. Roose had been planning the 'Red Wedding' massacre for some time. The morning after

Robb, his wife, his mother and other family members are all killed and their bannermen taken unawares and murdered in their beds, Roose makes clear the reasons for acting as he did: "He ignored my advice at every turn. If he'd been a trifle less arrogant ..." He doesn't finish the sentence but it's clear that he means that the bloodbath might have been avoided.

We've all been in meetings where the viewpoints differ so greatly that it seems unlikely that a conclusion will ever be reached. It can be very frustrating, but if your business suffers from fundamental division it can only survive for so long. Internal instability can cause a range of problems, from becoming a distraction that stops you from getting on with business to creating serious rifts that mean the company is pulled in several different directions at once. Research In Motion Limited (RIM), now known by the more familiar name BlackBerry, was an early mobile telecommunications innovator. Its principal selling point in an era when other phones offered only the ability to make calls and send text messages was its BlackBerry Messenger technology which enabled the devices to receive emails. This made it popular with businesses, who would give BlackBerrys to their executives so that they were contactable on the move. In 1999 BlackBerry's phones were the executive's choice and the company was riding high in its market, a position it managed to maintain for several years.

But then in 2007 a new product was launched – the iPhone. At first the executives at RIM didn't see it as much of a threat to their core market – the business customers – but as it became clear that the Apple product was taking chunks out of their business they realized something needed to be done. The problem was that they could not agree on what that should be. According to an article published in the *Wall Street Journal* in June 2012, one of the company's major stumbling blocks was fundamental differences between the two CEOs, who didn't even work in the same part of town, making meetings with both present a rarity. One of the co-CEOs, Jim Balsillie, believed they needed to diversify by licensing their technologies, including BlackBerry Messenger, to other platforms. On this he disagreed with the other CEO, Mike Lazaridis, who believed that the way forward was developing the phones themselves. Because of these unresolved differences Balsillie began to find his position untenable and left the company in January 2012. Mike Lazaridis became vice chairman and appointed a new CEO, Thorsten Heins, who cancelled Balsillie's licensing project to focus on product.

But even among those who thought the product needed to be updated there was disagreement. Lazaridis, the company's founder, was fixated on the clickable keyboard that people associated with the BlackBerry phones, and believed this differentiated them in a market awash with touch-screen phones. Heins, however, was insistent that to compete with Apple and Android BlackBerry needed to give people touch-screen smartphones with app capabilities. The product he launched, the Z10, contained all these features but unfortunately it was a massive flop. According to Canadian paper the *Globe and Mail*, the company reported a US$965-million second-quarter loss in September 2013 and the main culprit was the huge quantity of unsold Z10s. Over the five years from 2008 to 2013 BlackBerry's value dived by $75 billion, and in November 2013 Heins was sacked (though don't feel too sorry for him – he received a $22 million pay off).

Because of internal divisions BlackBerry was unable to take the action it needed and move quickly in a fast-paced market. By the time it did take action it found itself launching a touch-screen phone six years after the appearance of the original iPhone, and it was too late. Nobody was massacred and Black-Berry has so far survived, even posting a slight profit at the end of the first quarter in 2014, but it is no longer the market domi-nator it once was and a fundamental failure to agree played a huge part in that.

27

OPPORTUNITY FROM ADVERSITY

Tyrion Lannister: *"Death is so final ... whereas life, life is full of possibilities."*

When Bran is pushed from the tower window by Jaime he ends up in a coma. Having been brought up learning all the skills of a young lord he had dreamed of becoming a knight in the Kingsguard and a bannerman for his brother Robb. On waking he learns that he will never walk again and tells Robb that he would rather be dead than lame. Jaime suggests to Tyrion that Bran would be better off dead, but Tyrion counters that by being dead Bran would miss out on all the potential opportunities life has to offer. Having lived with the adverse circumstance of being a dwarf for his entire life Tyrion should know what he's talking about.

While Bran is recovering, and learning to get around with the aid of Hodor, he starts to have prophetic visions involving a guide in the shape of a three-eyed raven. Both his father's death and the sack of Winterfell are shown to him in the form of visions. He then discovers an ability to see the world through the eyes of his direwolf, Summer. When he meets the Reeds they explain to him that he is a warg, one who can enter the minds of animals and control them. The Reeds help him to understand and develop both his gifts. Bran is able to use his gift of controlling animals to save Jon Snow from the Free Folk scouts who have turned on him as a traitor and also to control Hodor and free himself from the clutches of Locke. The three-eyed raven tells Bran he has to come to him and gives clues to his location. When Bran finally finds him – in the form of a man who has become one with a weirwood tree (just go with it, OK?) – the raven tells him that he will help him find what he has lost. Bran thinks this means he will walk again but the raven says he never will. But he will fly.

While the noble houses of Westeros are battling each other and the Free Folk are heading south to escape the threat posed by the White Walkers Bran seems to be on an entirely different, more mystical, mission. Clearly he has been marked for greatness and will be important in whatever the final showdown is but what that will be is not yet clear. What is obvious is that, while Bran can never be a soldier his disability has led him to discover two valuable new skills which mean he can play a role that's probably more important than the one he would have played as a knight.

So what do you do if, like Bran, your expectations are forcibly changed – but you don't have magical powers? When adversity knocks you sideways and seemingly destroys all your carefully laid plans it can appear that your life is over, but as many people have proven, adversity can often be the change that signals a brand new exciting life. When RAF physical trainer Sean Rose broke his back in a skiing accident he thought his high adrenalin life was over. Astonishingly, the very day he learned he was paralysed from the waist down he started writing a list of sports he could still do. Since then he's won a gold medal for Britain in a World Cup downhill skiing race, become a world champion water skier and competed in the Paralympic skiing team. He has said, 'I've definitely achieved more than I would have if I hadn't had the accident and I look at life differently; it's more fulfilling, I can appreciate what I've got.' It's a common theme among Paralympians. A car crash at the age of seven ended Jessica Galli's gymnastic dreams but she has gone on to win seven medals for the US in Paralympic track events, including a gold in the women's 400m (T53) race, and now sees the car crash as a catalyst that enabled her to achieve greatness.

Redundancy too is clearly a life-changing event, but it need not be a career-ending disaster. Of course it is difficult to come to terms with; however vague your plans for the future you probably had certain career expectations and there is also a sense of rejection as you ask yourself 'why me?' But once you have gone through the initial shock, a life-changing event like this can be just that – life-changing – and in a very positive way. While there will still be bills to pay most countries have rules regarding statutory pay and some companies will exceed these requirements. Particularly if you have received a better than statutory redundancy pay-out it can allow you to take stock, work out what you really want to do, find a career with a company that shares your goals and values, change career completely or even become your own boss.

Larger companies may even offer career counselling as part of the redundancy package or you could independently consult one of the many career advisory companies available. A career consultant will sit down with you and try to understand not only what your strengths and weaknesses are but also what you want to get out of a job. It helps to get a fresh perspective – if you've worked in a particular role or industry for many years you may only be able to see yourself in that context. A professional assessing you more dispassionately could open you up to the possibility of a career you had never even considered.

There may well have been something you've always dreamed of doing – such as starting out again in a completely different industry or progressing your hobby into a business. In the past you may have been too scared to take the plunge, perhaps because you feared losing the security of your regular income. Now that security has been taken from you look at it instead as freedom gained – without fear of losing you can dare more. Bran will never walk again, but he will fly – could your dreams take wing too?

28

NOBODY LIKES A SMART-ARSE

Jon Snow: *"They hate me 'cause I'm better than they are."*

When Jon Snow turns up at Castle Black to join the Night's Watch it's far from what he expected. Instead of a rugged band of heroes defending the country from so-called Wildlings (their name for the Free Folk) and the White Walkers he finds a gaggle of criminals, rejects, waifs and strays. He's by far the best fighter among the latest batch of recruits, and has learned much in the way of strategy and leadership by being brought up alongside Lord Stark's legitimate children. To be honest he's a bit up himself; little wonder that to begin with he's generally unpopular with his fellow recruits, or that the Master at Arms, Ser Alliser Thorne, takes against him. Thorne's antipathy towards Jon sees him assigned to the stewards rather than the rangers and has all his ideas rejected by Thorne almost on principle. It's a warning to all "clever little twats" out there.

When Jon returns from his travels with the Wildlings he is tried in front of Night's Watch men including Ser Alliser and the recently arrived Janos Slynt. Janos was commander of the City Watch, the one who Ned thought he had on his side before realizing too late to keep his head that Janos had been bought off by somebody else. So he's no fan of Jon anyway, branding him the "bastard son of a traitor" and suggesting execution before they've even heard Jon's evidence. A sensible man might try to win round Slynt, but an impulsive, self-assured man? When Janos points out his experience, reminding Jon that he commanded the City Watch, Jon responds, "And now you're here: you must not have been very good at your job." Jon gets out of the experience with his life but is unable to get them to act on his suggestion that they send men to Craster's keep to kill the mutineers from the Watch before they can reveal Night's Watch secrets to Mance's men.

Because of his cockiness Jon now has two significant members of the leadership of the watch wishing him dead. It doesn't help that he has become popular with his peers. Though, as Sam admits, their jealousy of Jon's accomplishments might make them want to hate him, they can't. Janos points out to Ser Alliser that he is only acting commander of the Night's Watch and that when the time comes to choose a new commander it could easily be Jon since, "The bastard's well liked. You're not." There's a danger that they could soon be taking orders from Jon. He suggests that Ser Alliser allows Jon to march on Craster's and fight the mutineers. In all likelihood he'll be killed, which will save the two of them a lot of trouble.

Luckily for Jon he is as good as he believes himself to be and returns in time to prove himself a natural leader at the battle with the Wildlings at Castle Black. But if you behaved like this in a business context and treated those senior to you with such little respect the consequences would most likely be severe. Alliser Thorne is not a nice man, but he treats the troops roughly because he believes from experience that it's the only way to make them strong – weak and cowardly members threaten the safety of the whole team. At the age of only about 20, with no real-world experience, who is Jon to second guess him?

Yes, you may be clever, you may have bags of great ideas, you may be brilliant at everything you do but is it a good idea to let everybody know it all the time? How does it make them feel? Chances are if you act like this it'll inspire jealousy in your colleagues and any superior who feels undermined is likely to sideline you and shoot down all your suggestions. There are ways to impress more subtly and you'll get much better results from a more measured approach than you will by throwing your weight around and telling everybody why you're right (and your manager is wrong).

It isn't that young people can't lead; there are plenty of examples to contradict that, including those of Bill Gates and Mark Zuckerberg, both of whom started their companies while they were undergraduates (Harvard undergraduates, but young nonetheless). A young person can often bring a fresh perspective to a situation where more experienced people who think they've seen everything before might simply tread the same well-worn route. But in order to get yourself in a position where you can make your voice heard you need to play the game by their rules. Jon tries to get Alliser to take up his suggestion that they block the tunnels to prevent the Wildlings getting into Castle Black by shouting and arguing. At this point Ser Alliser is so sick of him Jon couldn't persuade him no matter how he tried and shouting only makes the acting commander more determined not to do what Jon wants. As Ser Alliser points out, if he gave into this kind of behaviour and let Jon's ideas make him doubt his own he'd completely lose authority.

So if shouting doesn't work what does? Well how about internal networking. Clearly this is a long-term approach and is not going to work in a situation where you've already made yourself unpopular. It should be a way of life for all serious careerists. Make sure you talk to the right people in your business, volunteer for extra-curricular working opportunities, show up at company social events (do not get drunk!) – even rehearse what you would say to the chief executive should you stumble across them in the elevator. Once you become a recognized name among those with the power to push through decisions you'll be in a better position to put your ideas across.

Now you have their ears you can use your influencing skills. Remember to put the suggestion in their language and show clearly how the company, and therefore the person you are influencing will benefit from it. If you can't tell them what's in it for them (kudos, more power, whatever they value) you've already hit a problem. Also take care to make your suggestion at the right time: your idea might be very important to you but they probably have plenty of other things on their minds. Finally, be clear what it is you are suggesting. You don't want to get this far only to have a meeting where you vaguely skirt around what it is you are talking about and those you meant to influence come away not understanding what you've suggested.

Of course, if you have, like Jon, already burned your bridges you could try the potentially risky make or break strategy of just going ahead and doing it anyway. It is, as they say, easier to ask for forgiveness than it is to ask for permission. Just don't come crying to us if it all backfires.

29

PUT YOUR RIVALRY ASIDE

Mance Rayder: *"Do you know what it takes to unite ninety clans, half of whom want to massacre the other half for one insult or another? ... I told them we were all going to die if we don't get south. 'Cause that's the truth."*

It never rains but it pours. Winter is coming, which is pretty bad on its own, then the king is killed and the country is plunged into civil war. If those two things weren't enough to contend with, a presumed long-dead foe, the White Walkers, has been gathering strength in the north ready to head south with the coming winter. As Jojen Reed notes, "the Night's Watch can't stop them", so sooner or later the Walkers and their armies of the dead are going to make it beyond the Wall and into the Seven Kingdoms. If the warring families don't get their act together there may be no Iron Throne left to win.

The Wall was originally built and the Night's Watch instigated in order to keep out the White Walkers. Unfortunately, over the thousands of years since its construction sightings of the White Walkers have died out completely. People in Westeros now think the Wall is there just to keep out the Free Folk, who they refer to as Wildlings, and because of this the Night's Watch has become a dumping ground for criminals rather than a body of skilled and noble warriors. King Beyond The Wall, Mance Rayder, knows there is strength in numbers and managed to unite the bickering and battling Free Folk through fear of the larger threat. As he points out, the ninety clans he's united speak seven different languages and would normally be engaged in fighting one another rather than uniting for a common goal. If Jojen is right and not only can the Night's Watch not stop the Walkers but neither can the kings of Westeros, it would seem that these noblemen are going to have to ally themselves not only with one another but also with the King Beyond The Wall if they are to stand any chance of survival. This seems unlikely when you consider that one of the existing key alliances – Lannister–Tyrell – is far less stable than it appeared. The Tyrells were responsible for killing Joffrey, but managed to get the blame put on Tyrion, thereby increasing the internal tensions in House Lannister.

Some competitors are worse than others; they threaten to obliterate all in their path. But what if instead of having to face several small competitors the behemoth has to face a united front, one single group? Perhaps that way you could all survive – and live to fight another day. Perhaps this is what Starbucks and PepsiCo had in mind when they formed an alliance to sell coffee-based soft drinks. The rise of coffee outlets like Starbucks in the early 1990s led to reduced business for soft drinks companies such as PepsiCo because of the greater choice of drinks for the consumer. At the same time Starbucks wanted to increase its consumer reach and strengthen its position against direct competitors (other coffee shops) by selling drinks in supermarkets and other retail outlets. To do this on its own would have been very difficult because its existent business model didn't include either the production capabilities or the distribution channels required. PepsiCo had both, plus a big rival that it needed to compete with – Coca Cola. The new milk-based coffee drinks they created together allowed PepsiCo an entry into a different avenue of the soft drinks market and gave Starbucks reach beyond its previous means.

In 2014 it was announced that IBM and Apple were entering into a partnership to provide computing solutions within the enterprise technology market. This might seem surprising given the mutual antipathy of the two companies, with a 1984 advert for Apple likening IBM to 'Big Brother' and trumpeting itself as the solution for halting IBM's world domination. But since then other common rivals have crept to the fore, the most obvious one being Microsoft, whose products are standard in most companies. Apple, on the other hand, is seen more as a retailer of computer solutions for leisure and media applications and has found it difficult to get a hold in the corporate market. By forming an alliance with IBM and creating business tools and solutions together it will be hoping to make inroads into this lucrative area. IBM will be able to tap into the portability and cool-value of Apple's devices. Mobility, in the shape of things like cloud computing, is changing the way people work and IBM has clearly seen the value of becoming involved with a pioneer in this area.

Whether it works remains to be seen. Although forming an alliance with a rival can be mutually beneficial it is also fraught with difficulty. While enjoying the new relationship one must be careful not to forget that you are still rivals. IBM and Apple have joined forces in the past; in the 1990s they and Motorola joined up to tackle the Microsoft threat, but when none of their assaults on Microsoft's dominance worked the alliance fell apart. Starbucks and PepsiCo on the other hand have continued to work together since the mid-nineties. Perhaps this success can be put down to the fact that they created a separate area for their joint activities called the North American Coffee Partnership, in which they were equal partners. So instead of the two companies trying to pursue different goals together they were able to keep the joint activities separate from the individual pursuits and the new venture was able to function almost as a separate company. This makes sense in terms of decision-making too, which can be notoriously difficult within an alliance as it becomes politically difficult for anybody to have the final say. They have continued to develop products together with the latest joint innovation being 'Fizzio', a range of drinks freshly carbonated in Starbucks stores.

Car manufacturers Suzuki and Volkswagen were, on the other hand, involved in a three-year dispute over their failed partnership. In 2010 they agreed to a partnership which combined shared technologies and access to markets that could have benefited both sides. But the alliance lasted less than two years, with no progress made towards sharing technologies or markets. Volkswagen took a 19.9% share in Suzuki, which Suzuki demanded back, but Volkswagen refused, claiming that Suzuki broke the terms of the agreement. Reports suggest that there were several factors at play in the partnership's failure including the size discrepancy of the companies (Volkswagen being by far the larger expected to dominate the relationship); disparate work cultures and a failure to clearly map the route their alliance would take.

So while partnerships can be very beneficial they are not something to be entered into lightly. Objectives, processes and working methods all need to be clearly mapped before an alliance can go ahead. And even then you'd be foolish to forget that you are rivals.

30

DEFY EXPECTATION

Petyr Baelish: *"That's what I know, that's what I am, and only by admitting what we are can we get what we want."*

Many characters in *Game of Thrones* are bound by duty to pursue a particular path. Cersei is expected to marry and breed, Jaime is expected to be a great leader who carries on the glory of his family name, Sansa is expected to keep quiet and marry the king's son even if he is a little sadist and Renly and Loras are supposed to marry women even though they'd rather spend quality time with each other. Lords are meant to fight, make decisions and lead and ladies are meant to do needlework, stay out of important matters and bear children. But what happens when somebody defies expectation? When a lady would rather be a lord?

When we first see Arya Stark she is embroidering – badly, unlike her older sister – and she's bored. Her brother Bran is outside shooting arrows at a target. He keeps missing, then takes aim and an arrow whizzes straight into the centre of the target, and we see it was fired by Arya. When the court comes to visit she's told off by her parents for trying to greet the royal party wearing a helmet. Jon has a sword called Needle made for her before she departs for King's Landing and he leaves for the Wall. Ned's initial reaction is to confiscate this from her but instead he decides to hire a tutor so she can at least learn how to use it properly. She asks him if she can be a lord one day but he explains her expected destiny, "You will marry a high lord and rule his castle and your sons shall be knights and princes and lords." Well gee, thanks Dad, that sounds great. Actually Arya simply states, "No, that's not me." When Ned is executed and Arya is forced to flee the city, Yoren of the Night's Watch makes her disguise herself as a boy. She has little problem convincing people she's not a girl and the only person to see through her disguise instantly is wily old Tywin Lannister. In many ways the War of the Five Kings is good for Arya as, in the chaos of war, what's normal and appropriate is less important than survival. This gives her the opportunity to see what it's really like to be a boy. She's good at it!

Being a non-girly girl in a man's world can actually be an advantage. People continually underestimate Arya because of both her gender and her youth. Brienne of Tarth has also found this to be the case. Men fail to take her seriously despite her armour, her size and the fact that she never jokes, allowing her to have the upper hand in combat. As Tyrion explains to Jon Snow when he's sulking about being a bastard (goodness knows why, it seems incredibly common to the extent they've even invented a naming system for it), name-calling only has an effect if you fight against it: "Never forget what you are – the rest of the world will not. Wear it like armour and it can never be used to hurt you." This is exactly what Brienne does – although she leaps to defend the good name of others there's no insult she hasn't heard about herself before so when people mock her their jibes simply bounce off her emotional armour in the same way their blows bounce off her actual armour. Her unusual status as the realm's only (as far as we know) female knight leads Cat Stark to entrust the important mission of Jaime's safe return to King's Landing to her. Brienne is one of the few characters who is not intent on personal glory. She does not play the game of thrones; her goal is to be a knight and serve a noble master. Although Renly and Cat are both now dead she continues to serve them, the former by aiming to avenge his death and the latter by finding her daughters and conveying them to safety.

The point is that Brienne and Arya would both arguably have easier lives if they did what was expected of them but while their struggle with the outside world might have been lessened their inner struggle would have been greater. They could have ended up married to great lords and produced further great lords but what kind of life is that for somebody with an active mind and skill as a fighter? One only has to look at Cersei to see what happens when an intelligent woman is forced into the role of political playing piece and bearer of great men – she becomes bitter, angry and vindictive, using her intelligence to make the lives of others worse.

'My Way' tops the list of favourite songs played at funerals. But when we look back at our careers how many of us will truly be able to say we achieved what we did without compromising our values or personality? The decision to do what you love regardless of the consequences is a tough one but what's worse: following your heart and failing or always wondering 'what if'?

Perhaps in your youth you had a particular hobby – writing, gardening, playing the spoons – pursuing it enthusiastically and becoming good at it. But then it was off to university with you, after which you had to do something worthy of your education so you joined Big Corp Inc. as a management recruit. You may have been slowly working your way up the company ladder with the expectation that eventually you'll win a place on the board. But if you've also discovered that each year a little piece of your soul has died and you constantly yearn to express yourself in writing, or your green fingers are itching uncomfortably, can you really call yourself 'successful'? Some people love the cut and thrust of business, they get a kick from it every day, but if you are constantly thinking 'if only ...' you're in the wrong job. It might be difficult to break away from the company lifestyle and its financial and status rewards but wouldn't you love to see what happens if you do it your way?

CONCLUSION

"A business book based on *Game of Thrones*? Surely that's a guide for how *not* to do business," is what one friend said when she was told about this book. And she's right, a lot of the actions taken by the characters in the series are questionable at best, and it is after all fiction, entertainment. But it is to be hoped that by reading this book and revisiting the series you have been able to learn from the mistakes made by the characters or found a new way of thinking about a particular problem in your career.

You will have seen that the amoral approach to success is not the only one. If taking a purely pragmatic approach to business, putting in the hours, doing whatever it takes, no matter how despicable, to achieve your ambitions worked then Tywin Lannister would have finished Season 4 striding round the throne room, not sitting in the privy with a couple of arrows in him. Tywin was a clever and charismatic man, a strategist who understood, generally, how people would react in particular circumstances. But he lacked the emotional intelligence to understand individuals. Because of this he really never considered that Tyrion, his own son, would refuse to sacrifice his future or even his life for the sake of the Lannister name, nor did he realise that when cornered Tyrion would find the strength to turn on him.

The highly moral Starks have come in for some stick in this book, which may seem to imply that those with high morals cannot succeed, can't win. That's not necessarily the case. The problem with the Starks is that their morals are all they have. They don't really stand for anything but simply stand against what is wrong, in this case the Lannisters. They aren't interested in ruling; Ned's not keen on being Robert's Hand and Robb takes on the role of King in the North with some reluctance. Both accept their missions because the alternative is seeing the country ruled by the power crazed. Take away the despots though and what do the Starks really represent?

So is there a way to be ambitious and take a pragmatic approach but still act morally? The example of Daenerys suggests there might be. She is morally upstanding, fighting for the weak, freeing slaves and punishing wrongdoers. She's ambitious but not in a selfish way – her desire for the throne is motivated by what's best for her country, not a personal hunger for power. But she is pragmatic too – freeing the slaves not only improves their lives but also makes her popular among the people, meaning that they will willingly fight for her when the time comes. Of course she's not perfect and her advisers have had cause to criticise some of her actions. For instance when she choses to crucify one master of Meereen for every child the masters had crucified, Barristan Selmy tells her, "Sometimes it is best to answer injustice with mercy" but she responds that she "will answer injustice with justice", proving that's she's also a decisive leader. Whether Daenerys will be the ultimate winner of the game remains to be seen – there are still the enigmatic Stannis Baratheon and the dastardly Lord Baelish to consider, never mind the advancing White Walkers, who could change the game completely – but it seems at the moment she offers the most realistic blueprint for success.

So take this book as food for thought, perhaps even use it as a jumping-off point for your next presentation. It'll certainly hold your colleagues' attention better than an interminable stream of PowerPoint slides.

SOURCES

Introduction
William H. Calvin, 'The Emergence of Intelligence', *Scientific American Presents* 9(4): 44–51 (November 1998)

Chapter 1
Nicole LaPorte, 'Rebooting YouTube', *Fast Company*, September 2014

Chapter 2
Walter Isaacson, 'The Real Leadership Lessons of Steve Jobs', *Harvard Buisiness Review*, April 2012

Chapter 3
Monica Lewinsky, 'Shame and Survival', *Vanity Fair*, June 2014

Chapter 5
Joel Faulkner Rogers, 'Public attitudes to the household energy market', YouGov.co.uk, 11 April 2014

Chapter 6

N. Gregory Mankiw, 'Defending the one per cent', *Journal of Economic Perspectives*, 27(3): 21–34 (Summer 2013)

Chapter 7

'New Report Finds More than a Quarter of CV Checks Reveal Inaccuracies', First Advantage press release (www.fadv.com), 22 September 2014

Frank Litsky, 'U.S. Olympic Chief Quits Over Her Lies On College Degrees', *New York Times*, 25 May 2002

Chapter 8

Deborah Swallow and Eilidh Milnes, *The Diversity Dashboard*, Infinite Ideas, 2013, p. 15

Chapter 9

Ivan Misner, 'Got Business Goals? – Connect with Those Who Can Help You!' (blog), ivanmisner.com, 9 June 2014

Chapter 11

Peri Pakroo, 'Improve Your Financial IQ', *Entrepreneur*, 19 August 2011

Chapter 12

Laurie Bennett, 'Fortune 1000 boards: an incestuous group', news.muckety.com, 26 March 2011

Chapter 13

Sean Farrell, 'What's next for Thomas Cook's high-octane former boss?', *Guardian*, 26 November 2014

James Gallagher, '"Arrogance" of ignoring need for sleep', www.bbc.co.uk, 12 May 2014

Chapter 15
'The 25 Best Inventions of 2014', *Time*, 20 November 2014

Chapter 19
Alex Ferguson, *My Autobiography*, Hodder Paperbacks, 2014, pp. 66–7

Chapter 21
Ellen Nakashima and Ann E. Marimow, 'Judge: NSA's collecting of phone records is probably unconstitutional', *Washington Post*, 16 December 2013

Chapter 22
Malcolm Gladwell, *David and Goliath: Underdogs, Misfits and the Art of Battling Giants*, Penguin, 2014, p. 6

Reed Hastings, 'An Explanation and Some Reflections', blog. netflix.com, 18 September 2011

Chapter 24
Burt Helm, 'How I Did It: James Dyson', *Inc.*, 28 February 2012

Paul B. Brown, 'Entrepreneurs Are "Calculated" Risk Takers – The Word That Can Be The Difference Between Failure And Success', www.forbes.com, 6 November 2013

Chapter 26
Will Connors, 'Multiple Missteps Led to RIM's Fall', *Wall Street Journal*, 28 June 2012

Sean Silcoff, Jacquie McNish and Steve Ladurantaye, 'Inside the fall of BlackBerry: How the smartphone inventor failed to adapt', *Globe and Mail*, 27 September 2013

Chapter 27
Laura Mitchell, 'Paralympian Sean Rose: "I've got a better life now than before I broke my back"', *Daily Express*, 15 April 2014

Jessica Galli, 'How I became a Paralympian' (blog), www.teamusa.org, 3 June 2013